GLENDALLOCH,

AND

OTHER POEMS,

BY THE LATE DR. DRENNAN.

Second Edition.

WITH

ADDITIONAL VERSES,

BY HIS SONS.

DUBLIN:
WILLIAM ROBERTSON, 23, UPPER SACKVILLE-STREET.
LONDON: SIMPKIN, MARSHALL, AND CO.
EDINBURGH: JOHN MENZIES.
BELFAST: H. GREER.
1859.

ORIGINAL PREFACE.

I AM well aware of the wide distinction between a poet, and a maker of verses. A young gentleman, just entering into the printing business, had asked me, once and again, to give him an occasion of showing the public his progress in the typographic art, and I have, at length, weakly, though not unwillingly, complied with his request. I gave him the following pieces, connected with past events, some by pleasant, but most of them by painful associations. Yet, thanks be to Him who has made us of such a nature, that past pleasures still live in memory, and that time seldom fails to soften the pains we have suffered, into a pensive, but not unpleasing remembrance. Thus are we disposed to make the best of this passable life, and when the hour of parting arrives, to bid the world— GOOD NIGHT.

I dedicate this little volume to my Wife, my Sisters, and my Children. To the last of whom I shall not hesitate to recommend the art of versifying, as, at all periods of life, an amiable, and even useful recreation; although, except in some rare instances, a painful, precarious, and very profitless vocation.

March 17th, 1815.   W. D.

MEMOIR.

WILLIAM DRENNAN, author of Glendalloch and other Poems in the first part of this volume, and of various political writings, was born in Belfast, on the 23rd of May, 1754. His father was the Rev. Thomas Drennan, a dissenting minister in that place; his mother, Anne Lennox, was co-heiress with an elder sister to a moderate landed property in the neighbouring county of Down. Of nine children, besides twins still-born, he was the youngest, and his birth, occurring after the deaths of five elder brothers, afforded some balm for his parents' repeated sorrows. His father died before the lad had completed his fourteenth year, but the filial love and reverence so early implanted, may be traced in the verses entitled "My Father."

The year after his decease, William entered Glasgow College, where he pursued his studies for three sessions, or terms, and in 1771 obtained the degree of Master of Arts. He then prosecuted the study of medicine in Edinburgh in the years 1773 to 1778, in the last of which he obtained his doctor's degree.

In 1781–2 he began to practise in his native town of Belfast, but, not succeeding according to his wishes, removed to Newry at the end of the latter year. There he continued till 1789, (in the December of which year he changed his residence to Dublin), with annually increasing success, not neglecting, however, the cultivation of literature, which he regarded as the sweet solace of his life. In this town, besides minor political articles, he wrote his "Letters of Orellana, an Irish Helot."

The latter part of the title is sufficiently indicative of the scope of the work, but this sketch is too brief to enter on such subjects, and the editor must restrict himself to facts connected with Dr. Drennan, and merely state his opinions when necessary to connect them with their consequences to himself, or to obviate the misconceptions of others. In the year 1778 he had entered " with ardent zeal," to use his own language, "into the first Volunteer Association made in this Kingdom, and was among the first, and among the last, in that ever-memorable institution."

At this time, or previously, his mind had become imbued with a conviction of the necessity of three great political measures—Catholic Emancipation, Parliamentary Reform, and, as a means, if not indeed the only means of procuring them, Union amongst Irishmen of every religious persuasion. To these objects he devoted the greater part of his life, and sacrificed what the world would call his interests. He did not survive to witness the accomplishment of either of the former, and had he lived to the present hour, the latter would have remained an unreality. Possibly the union with England permitted the former measures to be passed with some alleviation of the bitterness of party-spirit in Ireland, the field of battle, at least of debate, being at a distance. But in Dr. Drennan's day and country it was obvious that no good could be effected by the liberal party, unless it consisted of as many United Irishmen as possible, and his mind, therefore, conceived the idea of the society so denominated.

The preliminary details of forming the Belfast society were, in a considerable degree, entrusted to Theobald Wolfe Tone, the political agent of the Catholics; and when the editor expresses his conviction that the *idea* originated with Dr. Drennan, he has not the slightest wish to deprive Mr. Tone's memory of any merit which may attach to it among the friends of that cause, or to deny that he was sent to Belfast to constitute the first society, which adopted the name of United Irishmen, and which arose, as well as the first Volunteer Corps, in that town. That Dr. Drennan was the author of the Test adopted by the society, and of its principal publications, there can be no doubt whatever. Among them appeared, on the 14th December, 1792, an Address

from the Dublin Society of United Irishmen to the
Volunteers of Ireland, recommending them by the name
of Citizen Soldiers, "to resume the arms they had at
first taken up to protect their country from foreign
enemies and domestic disturbance."

That was not only too bold an address for the time,
and therefore eagerly seized on as "a pretext for re-
peated prosecutions," but it seems now to have been as
great an error as an attempt to galvanize a corpse,
long after the vital breath had departed.

It was represented by the crown lawyers as an
address to a body which existed only in their own
imaginations, if, indeed, even there, and which they
christened National Guards, as a connecting link with
revolution.   This splendid mendacity was probably only
intended to impose on the worshipful juries, but its inven-
tion was one of the last tributes of respect to the name
of Volunteer.   Not till the 25th of June 1794, there
having, however, been several intermediate prosecutions
of others, was Dr. Drennan tried for this "wicked and
seditious libel," to use the approved legal parlance.
He was defended by Curran, as his principal counsel,
who made probably a better speech than has been
reported, and such a cross-examination of the chief
witness for the crown as shattered his evidence so
completely, that the jury were "reluctantly compelled"
to return a verdict of Not Guilty, on which the court

rang with "indecent and vociferous plaudits." The editor believes that Dr. Drennan's connection with the United Irish Societies ended at or about this period; and that in those which led to the rebellion of 1798, he had no concern whatever. Without reference either to merit or demerit, the patriot of one party, or the traitor of another, he expresses no opinion, but it is his duty to publish what he conceives to be the truth, irrespective of either. In theory, Dr. Drennan was undoubtedly a Republican, and in practice would have preferred that form of government which approached most nearly to the actual, not virtual, representation of the people, in parliament. His mind seemed instinctively to grasp and assimilate every useful and liberal measure, and there have existed few men, if any, who had less subsequent cause to alter or even modify their early-formed opinions. He was an enthusiastic Irishman; but he was one of the first to see and to proclaim the faults of his countrymen. Against indolence, ignorance, and intemperance, no voice, having regard to his opportunities, was more loudly or constantly raised. He was the first, we believe, to christen the potato a lazy root; long ere modern tea-totalism, to show the evils of the Worm of the Still, and his whole life was a quiet crusade against bigotry and ignorance. It was not inconsistent in such a man to discourage an appeal to arms, as on his trial he was proved to have done, and

to dread one of the worst misfortunes to any country—
a civil war. An unsuccessful rebellion paved the way
for English gold, and Ireland, if not " conquered," was
certainly "purchased" by the neighbouring island.
Against that union Dr. Drennan, in common with other
Irishmen of higher position, and therefore of greater
notoriety, made an eloquent protest, but the bargain
had been made, the sale was completed, and Ireland
became an English province. In different words, a
province for the benefit of England; in other respects,
the island was so completely neglected, left so entirely
alien in its laws, customs, and habits; in the rela-
tion between landlord and tenant; in the comparative
barbarism of the Irish-speaking districts, and their
dependence upon the lazy root; left, in short, so com-
pletely Irish, that nearly half a century after its extinc-
tion as a country, a million and a half of its inhabitants
were swept away by a famine and emigration unexam-
pled among civilized nations.

That its interests should be postponed to those of
Britain was but natural, and was early foretold.
But such considerations did not weigh, in Dr.
Drennan's mind, half so heavily as the loss of all
Patriotic feeling; and in that respect he seems to have
been an innocent enthusiast, who would have provoked
only a smile in the present enlightened generation. In
his own person he was above even national prejudices,

Many of his friends were Scotch and English. Among the former, the Venerable Dugald Stewart; and he contracted an English union, in 1800, by marriage with a lady who still survives him. Of her it is enough, and little enough to say, that he could not have made a better choice of a help-mate for himself, or a mother for his children.

In 1807 he left Dublin,* to be nearer his sisters, in Belfast, and his northern property. After a short residence in that town he removed to a cottage, which had been built by his sister on a small farm, between two and three miles from Belfast. He joined Mr. Hancock, of Lisburn, a highly respectable and intelligent gentleman, of the most liberal sentiments, in the editorship of the *Belfast Magazine*, and took a lively interest in the educational welfare of that rapidly rising town. He was one of the first founders of the Academical Institution there, to which he contributed with heart and hand, time, purse, and pen. Indeed, so

* I regret to find an error in date in Dr. Madden's new edition of *Lives of United Irishmen*, respecting Dr. Drennan's removal to Belfast, which is made to occur in 1801 instead of 1807. This probably originated in a printer's mistake of the last figure, but I am sorry that Dr. M. did not find it convenient, or perhaps did not think it necessary, to send me a proof-sheet of this part of his work. His diligence and anxiety to procure accurate information, at considerable cost and trouble, make me doubly sorry that it was not in my power to furnish a correction, unimportant perhaps to the general reader; but which, among Dr. Drennan's family and friends, may appear to be essentially required.

attached was he to it, that in his last illness he directed
his coffin to be stayed on its way to the grave, for a
few moments, before its gates. He had never been a
robust man, and in the winter of 1819 his health began
seriously to decline. He removed, therefore, to his
sister's house, in Belfast, and after a period of con-
siderable suffering, from an affection, principally of the
liver, expired there on the 5th of February, 1820.
The journals of the day, even those of the most
opposite political opinions, spoke warmly in his praise.
His body was borne, according to his directions, by
six Protestants, and as many Catholics, to its resting-
place. There was no carriage at his funeral, but a
numerous attendance on foot, chiefly of the humbler
classes.

In person, Dr. Drennan was small (about five and
a-half feet), well proportioned, and active. In feature,
except the eyes, of a fine hazel hue, not remarkable
for comeliness or the contrary. In his youth, to
judge by a portrait left unfinished, notwithstanding
the expression which intellect generally emits, he
would have been considered plain. Naturally grave,
his smile, perhaps from its rarity, was very sweet.
In company, which he relished, he was extremely
agreeable, and even sportive, and to good female
society always partial. Abstinent in food, temperate
in drink, and in morals irreproachable, he was no

sour ascetic, or shunner of his fellow-men. An occasional diffidence in his own judgment would appear a failing to more presumptuous minds, and, perhaps, occasionally amounted to irresolution. Men of large views will not always see their path so clearly as those whose minds are cast in a narrower mould; but it were better, on the whole, to trust to the god within, than the fellow-mortal without them, for even his wide conceptions were sometimes straitened by association with others. Of scholarship he retained enough to gratify a cultivated mind, but his classical knowledge was probably, both in extent and accuracy, inferior to his father's. His prose style is elegant, but somewhat diffuse; in his political works, lively, ornate, and antithetical, it bears the stamp of the stirring times which produced it. His chief forte, however, in the editor's opinion, lay in the epistolary style; his letters are full of ease, wit, elegance, and light information, such as are generally accorded only to woman; many of them are also extremely interesting from their reference to public affairs, and remarkable persons, as well as from their exhibiting his own mind in its graver or lighter hues. But to the design of this little volume even extracts from his correspondence would be foreign, and were it not so, time and circumstances at present forbid their publication. His character, however, will be fairly enough drawn from his poems, especially that on himself.

One characteristic the editor refers to with filial gratitude—his father's great patience as an instructor. From him he derived his first acquaintance with the Latin tongue, and, subsequently, his taste for literature and partiality for liberal principles. From him, also, he learned not to be ashamed of his own country, or indifferent to the vicissitudes of others. He would fain endeavour to repay some little part of the debt which, under heaven, he owes to such a father, and his highest ambition would only seek not to be deemed wholly unworthy of him, while he is happy to know that there exists a far fitter representative, in the person of his younger brother—a second Dr. Drennan.

CONTENTS.

POEMS BY THE LATE DR. DRENNAN.

a

POEMS BY J. S. DRENNAN, M.D.

VERSES BY WILLIAM DRENNAN.

ERRATA

Page 68, Line 11 from bottom, *dele* "of."

„ 110, „   2 from bottom, "funeral," *read* "funereal."

„ 196, „   12 from top, *for* "bids," *read* "birds."

„ 197, „   14 from top, *for* "fring'd," *read* "fringéd."

„ 211, „   15 from bottom, *read* "its" surging white.

PREFACE.

THE plan of this little volume is novel; it may not be the worse on that account. I have often been asked, and at times somewhat reproachfully, for my father's poems, which have become very scarce. On looking them over, with a view to reprint them, several were found of merely temporary or local interest, and a few seemed unsuited for republication. A selection, however, proving insufficient to constitute a volume, my brother was applied to for a contribution; he most kindly assented to my request, and I have only to regret that his portion of the little book is not larger. To make up what was deficient in bulk, having secured some value, I have had recourse to my own desk, where, indeed, of quantity was found enough and to spare. Entertaining some doubts of the quality, versions from foreign authors of undisputed merit for the most part, have been generally preferred to anything—if, indeed, there was ought—that could be called original. The result is a "*Farrago libelli*," which will not, at least, be found destitute of variety. Verses by one hand are frequently monotonous, and in the editor's humble opinion, translations are somewhat undervalued. The English seem fond of whatever is old—even of old jokes—and that venerable one of everything suffering by translation—but a bishop, affords an overpowering argument against it. Yet even this opinion has been modified in favour of the Germans, for no other reason, that I am aware of, but this—that the Germans are good and faithful translators, and even the highest originals, Homer and Shakespeare, for example, are not found to suffer in such hands.

In Ireland, my friend, Dr. Anster, has returned the compliment to Germany in his admirable version of the first part of Faust.* If there be occasionally found there more than Goethé's words, it arises from an anxiety to elucidate and develop his meaning; and there is little, indeed, if anything, which the admirer of that remarkable poem would willingly part with.

After he had pioneered the then untrodden path, many rushed to the attack of the great German whose name is better known than pronounced, in England.

Among others, a very good translation of the same part, and perhaps better adapted for the Tyro, appeared from the pen of Miss Anna Swanwick, of London, with versions of several of his Dramas, as far as the writer can judge, very faithfully executed. At first sight,

* I trust we shall soon have the second part from the same pen.

indeed, few tasks would seem more facile than the faithful representation of a foreign author, at least where, as in the examples I have given, the translator understands the foreign language. But this is not so much a matter of course as the reader may imagine, for Scott and Shelley had a very small stock of German when they sate down to convert it into English, and comical consequences ensued—atoned for, indeed, by their high poetic powers. Where those powers are wanting, mere accuracy will not always supply their place. The spirit of the language, the style of the author, if possible the character of his mind, must be often caught or conceived, as well as his expressions faithfully rendered. Not merely verbally, as the very word he uses may have acquired a different shade of meaning, even in a cognate language. Without great care, therefore, there may be often too good a foundation for the old joke remaining applicable.

Of my own attempts, from various languages, I can be but an imperfect, even if a tolerably impartial judge. It will be seen by the scholar, that some are mere parodies, or paraphrases: the majority, however, I trust, may deserve the name of translations, in which the originals do not suffer to any agonizing degree by their change of costume.

The few Irish ballads, or sketches, were due, in a great measure, to the suggestion of the late Thomas

Davis, an enthusiastic Irishman, and even if overmuch
so, I at least could not blame him. He died too soon
to complete a ballad history of Ireland, but lived long
enough to inspire a very different mode of handling
Irish history from the fashionable, sneering, super-
cilious, Anglo-Irish cant of former days. About the
same time *The Annals of the Four Masters*, from the
Anglo-Norman invasion to the death of Elizabeth, were
published by an humble but enterprising bookseller,
Mr. Geraghty, of Dublin.

They afforded authentic information at an accessible
price, and a perfect blaze of Irish poetry, much of it of
too blood-red a hue, lit up the columns of *The Nation*.
Unfortunately the time had not yet arrived when Irish-
men of a certain temperament could look on the past
as past, and let bygones be bygones. A very extraor-
dinary melo-drama ensued, of which the editor will
only say that he hopes, for the welfare of his native
land, the curtain may have dropped on such exhibitions
for ever. Under the strong impression that we may at
length unite *God Save the Queen* and *St. Patrick's Day*,
which he has, perhaps, the bad taste to prefer to either
Partant pour la Syrie, or *Yankee Doodle*, or the far
finer *Marseillaise*—he has not scrupled to quote
passages of history, even where it appears to show
that the Irish have *not* "always fought badly at home."
He thinks, indeed, that they fought so well and so

long, that it may be about time to give it up, without
the slightest discredit, at least till there be something
worth fighting for, and somebody to fight against—
besides one another.

DUBLIN, *March*, 1859.

P.S.—As these remarks are going to press, we read
with some surprise and annoyance the alleged pro-
ceedings of supposed sane individuals, united under the
name of the Phœnix Society. A more domestic and
familiar species of fowl, whose step they have probably
practised, is irresistibly suggested to the imagination,
as a fitter emblem of such Patriots. In its wild state
it actually did afford a *Nom de Guerre* to men of similar
views; but it is submitted that the Stubble Bird is not
so volatile, and therefore a more respectable character,
and should be adopted, with, perhaps, the addition of
the Gridiron, in future, as an Emblem of Ireland,
"minimus natu." At the same time, such follies will
suggest to the provident Statesman the necessity of
leaving no apology for them in the laws of the country.
He will be but the more careful to outrage no class,
and no form of religious opinion, merely because he
may differ from them; to remember, that there may be
danger looming in a future war with a semi-Irish
America, unless the interests of the Irish Priest and
the Irish Farmer be consulted at home—in a word, he
will be *Just*, and Fear not.

DEDICATION

Of all and sundry the Stories in the third part of this
volume to Miss BESSY FRAZER, Cheltenham.

All my Castles in Spain Time has taken by sap,
   And my whiskers has left rather hoary,
At Fane Valley, since Bessy last lay in my lap,
   And look'd up in my eyes for a story.

When as stories enough it was hard to deliver,
   And Bessy had issued her ukase,
I stole the stout gossoon who never could shiver,
   And the frog, called Splish-splash, from the book-case.

How flatt'ring to find, when so far, far away,
   My story-bank drawn once again on ;
Tho' I fear I should scarcely know Bessy to-day,
   And thought she had forgot Daddy Drennan.

When the Daddy is gone, may some stories occur,
   (At present, perhaps, she won't heed them),
To remind her of one who inscribes them to her—
   And the rest, to whoever will read them.

I know how soon all will be laid on the shelf,
   Even those that may suit my young Fairy,
Which I send with my love—a big slice for herself—
   Yet enough for Eliza and Mary.*

* Miss Frazer's cousins, and the Author's very kind friends.

GLENDALLOCH,

AND

OTHER POEMS,

OF THE LATE DR. DRENNAN.

GLENDALLOCH.

1802.

Th' enchantment of the place has bound
All Nature in a sleep profound;
And silence of the ev'ning hour
Hangs o'er GLENDALLOCH's hallow'd tow'r; ([1])
A mighty grave-stone, set by Time,
That, 'midst these ruins, stands sublime,
To point the else-forgotten heap,
Where princes and where prelates sleep;
Where Tuathal rests th' unnoted head,
And Keivin finds a softer bed:
"Sods of the soil" that verdant springs
Within the sepulchre of kings.

HERE—in the circling mountain's shade,
In this vast vault, by Nature made,
Whose tow'ring roof excludes the skies
With savage Kyle's stupendous size;
While Lugduff heaves his moory height,
And giant Broccagh bars the light;

B

Here—when the British spirit, broke,
Had fled from Nero's iron yoke,
And sought this dreary dark abode,
To save their altars and their God,
From cavern black, with mystic gloom,
(Cradle of Science, and its tomb,)
Where Magic had its early birth,
Which drew the Sun and Moon to earth,
From hollow'd rock, and devious cell,
Where Mystery was fond to dwell,
And, in the dark and deep profound,
To keep th' eternal secret bound,
(Recorded by no written art,
The deep memorial of the heart,)
In flowing robe, of spotless white,
Th' Arch-Druid issued forth to light;
Brow-bound with leaf of holy oak,
That never felt the woodman's stroke.
Behind his head a crescent shone,
Like to the new-discover'd moon;
While, flaming, from his snowy vest,
The plate of judgment clasp'd his breast.
Around him press'd the illumin'd throng,
Above him rose the light of song;
And from the rocks and woods around
Return'd the fleet-wing'd sons of sound.

"MAKER OF TIME! we mortals wait
To hail thee at thy Eastern gate;
Where, these huge mountains thrown aside,
Expands for thee a portal wide.
Descend upon this altar, plac'd
Amidst Glendalloch's awful waste:
So shall the pæan of thy praise
Arise, to meet thy rising rays,

From Elephanta's sculptur'd cave,
To Eire, of the Western wave;
And the rejoicing earth prolong
The orbit of successive song:
For we by thy reflection shine—
Who knows our God, becomes divine.

"But ah! what dim and dismal shade
Casts this strange horror o'er the glade,
Causes e'en hearts of brutes to quake,
And shudders o'er the stagnant lake?
What demon, enemy of good,
Rolls back on earth this night of blood?
What dragon, of enormous size,
Devours thee in thy native skies?
O, save thy children from his breath,
From chaos, and eternal death!"

The Druid mark'd the destin'd hour—
He mounted slow yon sacred tow'r;
Then stood upon its cap sublime,
A hoary chronicler of time;
His head, amidst the deathful gloom,
Seem'd Hope, new-risen from the tomb;
And, while he rais'd to Heav'n his hand,
That minister of high command
The terrors of the crowd repress'd,
And smooth'd their troubl'd wave to rest—
Then spoke—and round the pillar'd stone
Deep silence drank his silver tone.

" He, who, from elemental strife,
Spoke all these worlds to light and life,
Who guides them thro' th' abyss above
In circles of celestial love,

Has this vast panorame design'd
A mirror of th' eternal mind.
To view of superficial eyes,
In broken points this mirror lies:
And knowledge, to these points apply'd,
Are lucid specks of human pride.
From beams of truth distorted, cross'd,
The image of our God is lost.
Those, only those become divine,
Who can the fractur'd parts combine:
Nature to them, and them alone,
Reflects from ev'ry part but ONE;
Their eagle eye, around them cast,
Descries the future from the past.
Justice will not annihilate
What Goodness did at first create.
The mirror, sully'd with the breath,
Suffers slight change—it is not death
That shadows yon bright orb of day:
See! while I speak, the orient ray
Breaks, sudden, thro' the darksome scene,
And Heav'n regains its blue serene.
And soon the mild propitious pow'r
Which consecrates the ev'ning hour,
Shall bend again her silver bow,
Again her softer day shall throw,
Smooth the dark brow of savage Kyle,
And grim Glendalloch teach to smile.
Now, Druids, hail the joyous light;
Fear God—be bold—and do the right."

He ceas'd—their chorus, sweet and strong,
Roll'd its full stream of sainted song.

"O! fountain of our sacred fire,
To whom our kindred souls aspire,

(Struck from the vast chaotic dark,
As from these flints we strike the spark,)
Thou Lord of Life and Light and Joy,
Great to preserve, but not destroy,
On us, thy favor'd offspring, shine!
Who know their God must grow divine.
And when thy radiant course is done,
Thou, shadow of another sun,
Shalt fade into his brighter sky,
And time become eternity."

But past, long past, the DRUID reign;
The CROSS o'ertopt the Pagan fane.
To this remote asylum flew
A priesthood of another hue;
More like the raven than the dove,
Tho' murm'ring much of faith and love.

A lazy sullen virtue slept
O'er the dull lake: around it crept
·The self-tormenting anchorite,
And shunn'd th' approach of cheerful light;
Yet darkly long'd to hoard a name,
And in the cavern grop'd for fame.
Where Nature reign'd, in solemn state,
There Superstition chose her seat;
Her vot'ries knew, with subtle art,
Thro' wond'ring eyes to chain the heart;
By terrors of the scene, to draw
And tame the·savage to their law,
Then seat themselves on Nature's throne,
And make her mighty spell their own.
The charming sorc'ry of the place
Gave Miracle a local grace;
And, from the mountain-top sublime,
The Genius of our changeful clime

A sort of pleasing panic threw,
Which felt each passing phantom true.

E'en at a more enlighten'd hour
We feel this visionary pow'r;
And, when the meanest of his trade,
The ragged minstrel of the glade,
With air uncouth, and visage pale,
Pours forth the legendary tale,
The Genius, from his rock-built pile,
Awful, looks down, and checks our smile.
We listen—then a pleasing thrill
Creeps thro' our frame, and charms our will,
'Till, fill'd with forms fantastic, wild,
We feign—and then become the child.

We see the hooded fathers take
Their silent circuit round the lake:
Silent—except a wailful song,
Extorted by the leathern thong.

Cronan, Cornloch, Lochaun, Doquain,
Superiors of the servile train,
Envelop'd in their cowls, they move,
And shun the God of Light and Love.

Who leads the black procession on?
St. Keivin's living skeleton,
That travels through this vale of tears,
Beneath the yoke of six score years;
Sustains his step a crozier wand;
Extended stiff one wither'd hand,
To which the blackbird flew distress'd,
And found a kind protecting nest;
There dropt her eggs, while outstretch'd stood
The hand—till she had hatched her brood\

Hark! what a peal, sonorous, clear,
Strikes, from yon tow'r, the tingling ear!
(No more of fire the worship'd tow'r;
The holy water quenched its pow'r.)
And now, from every floor, a bell
Tolls Father Martin's funeral knell,
Who slipt his foot on holy ground,
And plunged into the lake profound;
Or, by the load of life oppress'd,
Sought refuge in its peaceful breast.

What!—Did not peace, delighted, dwell
The hermit of the mountain cell?

No—'twas a cage of iron rule,
Of pride and selfishness the school,
Of dark desires, and doubts profane,
And harsh repentings, late, but vain;
To fast—to watch—to scourge—to praise
The golden legend of their days;
To idolize a stick or bone,
And turn the bread of life to stone;
Till, mock'd and marr'd by miracles,
Great Nature from her laws rebels,
And man becomes, by monkish art,
A prodigy—without a heart.
No friend sincere, no smiling wife,
The blessing and the balm of life;
And knowledge, by a forged decree,
Still stands an interdicted tree.—
Majestic tree! that proudly waves
Thy branching words, thy letter leaves;—
Whether, with strength that time commands,
An oak of ages, Homer stands,

Or Milton, high-topt mountain pine,
Aspiring to the light divine;
Or laurel of perennial green,
The Shakespeare of the living scene,—
Whate'er thy form—in prose sublime,
Or trained by art, and prun'd by rhyme,
All hail, thou priest-forbidden tree!
For God had bless'd, and made thee free.
God did the foodful blessing give,
That man might eat of it, and live;
But they who have usurp'd his throne,
To keep his Paradise their own,
Have spread around a demon's breath,
And named thee Upas, tree of death.
Thy root is Truth, thy stem is Pow'r,
And Virtue thy consummate flow'r.
Receive the circling nations' vows,
And the world's garland deck thy boughs!

From the bleak Scandinavian shore
The DANE his raven standard bore:
It rose amidst the whitening foam,
When the fierce robber hated home;
And, as he plough'd the wa'try way,
The raven seem'd to scent its prey;
Outstretch'd the gloomy om'nous wing,
For feast of carnage war must bring.
'Twas HERE the Christian savage stood,
To seal his faith in flame and blood.
The sword of midnight murder fell
On the calm sleeper of the cell.
Flash'd thro' the trees with horrid glare
The flames—and poison'd all the air.
Her song, the lark began to raise,
As she had seen the solar blaze;

But, smote with terrifying sound,
Forsook the death-polluted ground;
And never since, these limits near,
Was heard to hymn her vigil clear.

This periodic ravage fell,
How oft, our bloody annals tell!
But ah, how much of woe untold,
How many groans of young and old,
Has Hist'ry, in this early age,
Sunk in the margin of her page,
Which, at the best, but stamps a name
On vice, and misery, and shame.

Thus flow'd in flames, and blood, and tears,
A lava of two hundred years;
And though some seeds of science seen,
Shot forth, in heart-enliv'ning green,
To clothe the gaps of civil strife,
And smooth a savage-temper'd life,
Yet soon new torrents black'ning came,
Wrapt the young growth in rolling flame,
And, as it blasted, left behind
Dark desolation of the mind.

But now no more the rugged North
Pours half its population forth;
No more that iron-girded coast
The sheath of many a sworded host,
That rush'd abroad for bloody spoil,
Still won on hapless Erin's soil,
Where Discord wav'd her flaming brand,
Sure guide to a devoted land;
A land, by fav'ring Nature nurs'd,
By human fraud and folly curs'd,

Which never foreign friend shall know,
While to herself the direst foe!

Is that a friend, who, sword in hand,
Leaps, pond'rous, on the sinking strand,
Full plum'd, with ANGLO-NORMAN pride—
The base adult'rer by his side
Pointing to Leinster's fertile plain,
Where (wretch!) he thinks once more to reign?
Yes, thou shalt reign, and live to know
Thy own, amid thy country's woe!
That country's curse upon thy head,
Torments thee living, haunts thee dead;
And, howling thro' the vaults of Time,
E'en now proclaims and damns thy crime:
Six cent'ries past, her curse still lives,
Nor yet forgets, nor yet forgives
DERMOD, who bade the Normans come
To sack and spoil his native home.

Sown by this traitor's bloody hand,
Dissension rooted in the land;
Mix'd with the seed of springing years,
Their hopeful blossoms steep'd in tears—
And late posterity can tell
The fruitage rotted as it fell.

Then Destiny was heard to wail,
While on black stone of INISFAIL
She marked this nation's dreadful doom,
And character'd the woes to come.
Battle, and plague, and famine plac'd
The epochs of th' historic waste;
And, crowning every ill of life,
Self-conquer'd by domestic strife.

Was this the scheme of mercy, plann'd
In ADRIEN's heart, thro' HENRY's hand,
To draw the savage from his den,
And train the IRISHRY to men,
To fertilize the human clay,
And turn the stubborn soil to day?
No—'twas two Englishmen, who play'd
The mas'try of their sep'rate trade:
Conquest was then, and ever since,
The real design of priest and prince;
And, while his flag the king unfurl'd,
The father of the Christian world
Bless'd it, and hail'd the hallow'd deed—
For none but SAVAGES would bleed;
Yet, when these savages began
To turn upon their hunter, man—
Rush'd from their forests, to assail
Th' encroaching circuit of the pale—
The cause of quarrel still was good;
The ENEMY must be subdued.

Subdued! The nation still was gor'd
By law more penal than the sword;
Till Vengeance, with a tiger start,
Sprang from the covert of the heart.
Resistance took a blacker name,
The scaffold's penalty and shame;
There was the wretched REBEL led,
Uplifted there the TRAITOR's head.

Still there was hope th' avenging hand
Of Heav'n would spare a hapless land;
That days of ruin, havoc, spoil,
Would cease to desolate the soil;
Justice, tho' late, begin her course,—
Subdued the lion law of force.

There was a hope, that, civil hate
No more a policy of state,
Religion not the tool of pow'r,
Her only office, to adore—
That Education, HERE, might stand,
The harp of Orpheus in her hand,
Of power t' infuse the social charm,
With love of peace and order warm,
The ruder passions all repress'd,
And tam'd the tigers of the breast,
By love of country and of kind,
And magic of a master mind.

As from yon dull and stagnant lake
The streams begin to live, and take
Their course thro' Clara's wooded vale,
Kiss'd by the health-inspiring gale,
Heedless of wealth their banks may hold,
They glide, neglectful of the gold,
Yet seem to hope a Shakespeare's name
To give *our* Avon deathless fame;
So, from the savage barren heart,
The streams of science and of art
May spread their soft refreshing green,
To vivify the moral scene.

O, vanish'd hope!—O, transient boast!
O, country, gain'd but to be lost!
Gain'd by a nation, rais'd, inspir'd,
By eloquence and virtue fir'd,
By trans-atlantic glory stung,
By GRATTAN's energetic tongue,
By Parliament that felt its trust,
By Britain—terrify'd and just.
Lost—by thy chosen children sold;
And conquer'd—not by steel, but gold:

Lost—by a low and servile great,
Who smile upon their country's fate,
Crouching to gain the public choice,
And sell it by their venal voice.
Lost—to the world and future fame,
Remember'd only in a name,
Once in the courts of Europe known
To claim a self-dependent throne.
Thy ancient records torn, and tost
Upon the waves that beat thy coast;
The mock'ry of a mongrel race,
Sordid, illiterate, and base.
To science lost, and letter'd truth ;
The genius of thy native youth,
To Cam, or Isis glad to roam,
Nor keep a heart or hope for home :
Thy spark of independence dead ;
Thy life of life, thy freedom, fled.

Where shall her sad remains be laid ?
Where invocate her solemn shade ?

HERE be the mausoléum plac'd,
In this vast vault, this silent waste ;—
Yon mould'ring pillar, 'midst the gloom,
Finger of Time ! shall point her tomb ;
While silence of the ev'ning hour
Hangs o'er Glendalloch's ruin'd tow'r.

WISH.

Amid the gently rippling waves,
 Like one of angel kind,
The snow-white swan glides on, and leaves
 A track of light behind ;

Emblem of pure and honest fame,
  Still hallow'd by retreat,
That swims, unsullied by a stream
  Which only laves the feet.

Sequester'd lives the prophet-bird;
  But, when it comes to die,
A sweet melodious note is heard,
  Glad presage of the sky!

Oh that the same prophetic pow'r
  To dying man were given!
Then might I hail the parting-hour,
  With augury of Heaven.

———

FRAGMENT OF SOPHOCLES.

There is One God, and there is only One;
The world he made must worship Him alone,
Whose breath creates, sustains, directs the whole,
The earth, air, ocean, and the human soul.
Yet wretched man, still arrogant, though blind,
Would soothe this God as one of human kind.
Will gold, or brass, or ivory, or stone,
That frame the idol, for the crime atone?
Or smoke of sacrifice, or bullock's blood
The sinner change to holy, just, and good?
Are such the means to free this world from evil,
To make of God, a man; of man, a devil?

FROM EURIPIDES.

Soul-soothing sleep, thou universal cure,
Health of the sick, and riches to the poor,
Come in thy cloud divinely bland and kind,
Immerse me wholly in a night of mind.
Yet through that night quick-gliding from afar
The dream may radiate as the evening star.
O'er my lone couch extend thy healing hand,
And gracious wave thy soporific wand;
Around these throbbing temples circumfuse
Thy balm oblivious, and thy dulcet dews,
This world dismiss'd with all its sordidness,
Oh bring me dreams at least of happiness!

FROM EURIPIDES.

Earth, in her vast expanse, recumbent lies,
She feels the ardour of th' embracing skies,
In genial show'rs descends prolific Jove,
Impregnates earth, and all the air is love.
As if they fell with the soft-falling rain,
Lo fruits, lo flowers, lo fields of food-ful grain!
And ev'ry animal, or tame, or wild,
And man, of heav'n and earth the noblest child.
And hence this "Era" we with justice call
The mighty mother, and the nurse of all;
These spring from her, and these to her return,
She is their cradle, and, at last, their urn.
Of all conceived in her capacious womb,
Earth, in a few short years, becomes the tomb;
Yet *what* at first descended from the skies,

Again to Jove, the heav'nly father, flies,
Nothing that he gives birth to ever dies;
Scatter'd, not lost, nor yet to chaos hurl'd,
But still endures—the atom, or the world.

———

DEATH OF ADONIS, FROM BION.

Ah! see the beautiful Adonis, lying
Outstretch'd on mountain-top, and dying—dying!
Gored in the thigh by that accursed Boar,
With tusk not whiter than the skin it tore;
Ah! see the blood, in purple stream fast-flowing,
Adown the snowy skin in gushes going;
Ah! see his manly breast with pain upheaving,
And life in short quick pants just leaving—leaving!
Ah! see the rose upon his lips now fading,
And his dim eyes the clouds of death pervading.
Mournful and mute his comrades stand before him,
And Venus, Venus, hovers madly o'er him.
Warm kisses now she gives, as life inspiring,
Then tremulous and weak, the kiss itself expiring.
She feels the kiss to his cold cheek applying,
Unknown, unfelt, by poor Adonis dying.
With arms high-arch'd she stood, at first astounded,
Then shriek'd aloud, as though herself were wounded;
Stay, dear Adonis, 'tis thy Venus holds thee,
Venus, who in her arms thus longingly enfolds thee,
Take, my Adonis, take this last embracing,
Let our lips mix in softest interlacing!
Alas, thou fleest me, fast and far descending,
To mix, a shade, with shadows never ending.
Ah, could I yield thee my divinity,
Then thou wouldst stay, or I might follow thee.

Take him, Persephone, he is thine own;
How will the beauteous youth adorn thy throne!
All that is beautiful devolves to thee,
All that is wretched now remaims with me;
Far, far superior is thy power to mine,
Oh! were I mortal more, or more divine;
Adonis dead, now love is but a name;
Beauty, illusion; and desire, a dream.

HAMILCAR, THE LION.

Oh, dear native land, oh, lost Irish nation,
The day is now come of thy great subjugation;
Thy branches are broken, thy leaves are off-shaken,
Thy roots are uptorn, and thou art forsaken.
In vain, by the bounty of God thou'rt befriended,
Cruel man hath still marr'd what kind nature intended;
By the flame, by the sword, by the scourge thou'rt
    instructed,
And thus to a marriage with England conducted.

"My boy, wet thy hands in the blood of the altar!
In the oath that I give let thy tongue make no falter,
Here, stand on my helmet thou shortly shalt try on,
And prove thyself a whelp of Hamilcar the Lion.

You must fight, you must bleed, you must play the
    valiant foeman,
To quell the robber of this earth, the just and upright
    Roman,
Who in war or in peace breathes vengeance eternal,
And calls all freedom, but his own, conspiracy infernal.

Meted out, trodden down, and devour'd by the stranger,
For my country I've fought, I have faced ev'ry danger;
Now, God of our fathers, inspire this, my scion,
With a heart that can hate, like Hamilcar the Lion.

For our wrongs felt from Rome, and what's worse, our
  dishonour,
An old warrior's curses lie heavy upon her!
Now swear that you'll never forget nor forgive her;
His gloomy brow gleam'd, while his boy echoed—
  Never!

How truly he kept to that strict obligation,
Fields of Cannæ and Thrasymene tell each proud
  nation,
Tell how fortune him favours who farthest dare ven-
  ture;
That pow'rs great abroad, are oft weak at the centre.

But oh, dear native land, oh, lost Irish nation,
Shall such avenger rise to avert thy subjugation;
To show in kindred blood, a Carthagenian daring,
And if not born to conquer, at least to die for Erin!

———

ON THE EYE.

FROM A POEM WRITTEN IN HIS 21ST YEAR.

[*Published in Belfast Newsletter*, 14th *December*, 1774.]

Divinest sight, whose aid alone
Can make the universe our own;
Can break our chains to things below,
And wide creation wider show;
Can force the senses' destined goal,
Sublime diffuser of the soul.

And not to narrow laws confined,
Waft round the Omnipresent mind;
Best emblem of each purer thought,
Fresh spring, with rich ideas fraught,
Oh who can tell their endless store?
Ev'n Milton could their loss deplore.
The thoughts we fondly wish to hide,
Through these pellucid windows glide;
The look relaxed, the tyrant's glare,
The silly, saunt'ring, sodden stare;
The antic glow-worm's fairy flame
That twinkles with unmeaning gleam;
The bland elusive ev'ning ray,
Gilding the eye with dubious day;
The brilliant brown, the inky blot,
The little sportive azure spot;
The sapient, keen, energic fires,
Which wing'd philosophy inspires,
With calm contentment's halcyon eye,
The leer that should evoke a sigh,
Audacious anger's meteor blaze,
Meek mercy's supplicating gaze;
Each master passion of the breast
In these pure symbols shines confest.

TO

A YOUNG LADY,

FROM HER GUARDIAN SPIRIT.

Maid much belov'd! to Heav'n-sent truth attend,
A spirit speaks, but listen to the friend.
That Guardian Angel, whose unwearied care
Form'd thee so pure, and fashion'd thee so fair;

Who, like the wall of Paradise, arose,
To guard thee safe, amid surrounding foes;
Who left his Heav'n, to point thee out the road,
Regain'd it in thy mind, and made it his abode.
That spirit speaks—and, oh! be free from dread,
That spirit hovers o'er thy honour'd head,
Looks down, with ever new delight, to find
His image beaming from thy spotless mind.

My form I might reveal, and flash to sight,
In all the living majesty of light;
My ample wings expand, and fill the room
With splendor of high Heav'n, with Eden's lost perfume;
Entranc'd in light, o'erwhelm'd with ardent gaze,
Thy sense would shrink, and shun the vivid blaze;
My flow'r would droop, or vainly seek to shun
The scorching radiance of the parent sun.
Th' event I fear, and hide myself in shade,
Unseen the angel, unabash'd the maid.
List then, oh! lovely maid, to truth attend,
Forget the angel, but believe the friend.

When on thy lips the unfledg'd accents hung,
And feebly flutter'd on thy falt'ring tongue,
When still in motion, sweetly vagrant still,
Thro' its blest Eden, flow'd life's little rill:
With fresh supplies I fed its babbling tide,
And clear as crystal made the current glide;
Sweet flow'rs sprung up, profuse, where'er it came,
And constant sunshine sparkled on its stream.

Old Time stood wond'ring, while the fearless child
Play'd with his lock, and at his wrinkles smil'd:
And as he gaz'd intent, the frolic Hours,
Stole his broad scythe, and hid it deep in flow'rs.

Thus blest of Heav'n, thy op'ning beauties grew,
The passing year still added something new:·
You caught the mantle as the prophet flew.

I saw thy virtues take their morning flight,
And spread their wings to catch the liquid light:
Bright'ning they rose, with Heav'n's own lustre crown'd,
Then fearful dropt from high, and sought the humble
    ground.

I saw the new-born thought, in words not drest,
Cling, like a blushing infant, to thy breast:
I see it now, as Venus from her wave,
Wishing to leave it, yet afraid to leave,
Sweetly it turns the half-seen form away,
And gently bends to shun the gaze of day.

'Twas I who sent thy ever-varying dreams,
That rose like clouds illum'd by Fancy's beams;
And sail'd along, (my breath th' impelling wind,)
Thro' the clear azure of thy settled mind;
And some I sent to raise thy transient fears,
Then touch'd thee with my wand, and saw thee wake
    in tears.
I make th' angelic voice so sweetly rise,
Swell the bold note, and lift it to the skies.
O luxury of sound! to one alone,
That one a parent, luxury unknown;
Pensive she sits, while music floats around,
And sometimes starts, as if she heard the sound;
The sound still flutters o'er, and fears to rest,
Like some small songster, o'er its ruin'd nest;
When, now too sad to sing, too weak to fly,
It utters one shrill note, and lights—to die.

But let no cloud o'ercast thy dawning day,
Thy mother listens to a softer lay.

To sweeter sounds, to music more refin'd—
She listens to the harmony of mind.
That harp of God to its Creator plays,
Her life, an Alleluiah in his praise.
Music the angel in the breast must hear,
While his soft whispers soothe her mental ear.
Music responsive to those notes alone,
Which swell, enraptur'd, round the sapphire throne.

Sweet Maid, attend, the fleet-wing'd minute flies,
Destin'd to waft me to my native skies.
Thy Genius leaves thee, but he leaves behind,
Prudence—best guardian to th' obedient mind:
At her sage call, the vagrant passions fly,
Crowd round her parent wing, and cow'ring lie;
Compell'd by pow'r supreme to Heav'n I bear
The charge which Heav'n committed to my care:
Should I then grieve to make thy virtues known?
To make th' applauses of all worlds thy own?
My lyre, in joy, shall speak its sweetest lays,
My wings diffuse the richest dew of praise.
Yet whence this weight? My languid wings move slow—
I strike my lyre, it sounds the note of wo—
Slowly I rise to Heav'n—sweet Eden smiles below.

I shall return, to catch thy parting breath,
To gild the grave, and blunt the dart of Death;
In bright procession make thy virtues pass,
While Mem'ry looks, and Fancy holds the glass.
When life's last light shall tremble in thine eyes,
And cease to animate these crystal skies,
Then shall these virtues pour the cheering ray,
To decorate the setting of thy day.
The dazzling glories of the day may fade—
The crescent, Hope, shall rise, and brighten with the
    shade.

Thy faults!—where are they?—Angels cannot name:
A slight smoke hovers o'er a vestal flame,
Which grows more bright, illumed by Mercy's ray,
And as it mounts to Heav'n, it melts away.

O Thou! who on yon pole-star sit'st sublime,
To mark the lapse of ever-rolling Time,
I feel thy call——

Ann. Ætat. 18.

ERIN.

When Erin first rose 'from the dark-swelling flood,
God bless'd the green island, He saw it was good:
The Emerald of Europe, it sparkled, it shone,
In the ring of this world the most precious stone!

In her sun, in her soil, in her station, thrice blest,
With back turn'd to Britain, her face to the West,
Erin stands proudly insular, on her steep shore,
And strikes her high harp to the ocean's deep roar.

But when its soft tones seem to mourn and to weep,
The dark chain of silence is cast o'er the deep;
At the thought of the past, tears gush from her eyes,
And the pulse of the heart makes her white bosom rise.

" O, sons of green Erin! lament o'er the time
When religion was—war, and our country—a crime;
When men, in God's image, inverted his plan,
And moulded their God in the image of man.

" When the int'rest of state wrought the general woe;
The stranger—a friend, and the native—a foe;
While the mother rejoic'd o'er her children distress'd,
And clasp'd the invader more close to her breast.

" When with pale for the body, and pale for the soul,
Church and state join'd in compact to conquer the whole;
And while Shannon ran red with Milesian blood,
Ey'd each other askance, and pronounc'd it was good!

" By the groans that ascend from your forefather's grave,
For their country thus left to the brute and the slave,
Drive the Demon of Bigotry home to his den,
And where Britain made brutes, now let Erin make men!

" Let my sons, like the leaves of their shamrock, unite,
A partition of sects from one footstalk of right;
Give each his full share of this earth, and yon sky,
Nor fatten the slave, where the serpent would die!

" Alas, for poor Erin! that some still are seen,
Who would dye the grass red, in their hatred to green!
Yet, oh! when you're up, and they down, let them live,
Then, yield them that mercy which they did not give.

" Arm of Erin! prove strong; but be gentle as brave,
And, uplifted to strike, still be ready to save;
Nor one feeling of vengeance presume to defile
The cause, or the men, of the EMERALD ISLE. (⁷)

" The cause it is good, and the men they are true;
And the green shall outlive both the orange and blue;
And the daughters of Erin her triumph shall share,
With their deep-bosom'd chests, and their fair-flowing
hair.

"Their bosoms heave high for the worthy and brave,
But no coward shall rest on that soft-swelling wave;
Men of Erin! awake, and make haste to be blest!
Rise, Arch of the ocean, rise, Queen of the West!"

VERSES

FOR AN OLD IRISH MELODY.

[Supposed to be sung by the Females, after the event of an unfortunate battle; dissuading their remaining relatives from emigration.]

Alas! how sad, by Shannon's flood,
  The blush of morning sun appears!
To men, who gave for us their blood,
  Ah! what can women give but tears!

How still the field of battle lies!
  No shouts upon the breezes blown!
We heard our dying country's cries—
  We sit, deserted and alone!

Why thus collected on the strand,
  Whom yet the God of mercy saves?
Will ye forsake your native land?
  Will ye desert your brothers' graves?

Their graves give forth a fearful groan—
  "O, guard our orphans and our wives!
Like us, make Erin's fate your own,
  Like us, for her yield up your lives!"

Why, why such haste to bear abroad
   The witness of your country's shame?
Stand by her altars, and her God,
   He yet may build her up a name.

Then should her foreign children hear
   Of Erin, free and blest once more,
Will they not curse their fathers' fear,
   That left too soon their native shore?

PRESENTIMENT.

"There is a hopeless, bitter grief,
   Which oft the feeling heart must prove;
There is a pang that mocks relief;
   'Tis deep, consuming, secret love."

No sigh is heard, nor seen a tear,
   And strange to see a smile prevail!
But faint the smile, and insincere,
   And o'er a face so deadly pale!

This fairy dream of life is o'er,
   No visionary hope to save!
If Heaven a mercy has in store,
   O! send her to an early grave!

THE WORM OF THE STILL.

I have found what the learn'd seem'd so puzzled to tell—
The true shape of the Devil, and where is his Hell;
Into serpents, of old, crept the Author of Ill,
But Satan works now as a Worm of the Still.

Of all his migrations, this last he likes best:
How the arrogant reptile here raises his crest!
His head winding up from the tail of his plan,
Till the worm stands erect o'er the prostrated man.

Here, he joys to transform, by his magical spell,
The sweet milk of the Earth to an essence of Hell,
Fermented our food, and corrupted our grain,
To famish the stomach, and madden the brain.

By his water of life, what distraction and fear;
By the gloom of its light, what pale spectres appear!
A Demon keeps time on his fiddle, finance,
While the Passions spring up in a horrible dance!

Then prone on the earth, they adore in the dust,
A man's baser half, rais'd, in room of his bust.
Such orgies the nights of the drunkard display,
But how black with ennui, how benighted his day!

With drams it begins, and with drams must it end;
A dram is his country, his mistress, his friend;
Till the ossify'd heart hates itself at the last,
And the dram nerves his hand for a death-doing blast.

Mark that mother, that monster, that shame, and that
    curse!
See the child hang dead drunk at the breast of its nurse!

As it drops from her arm, mark her stupify'd stare!
Then she wakes with a yell, and a shriek of despair.

Is this the civility promis'd our nation?
This the Union—dissolv'd in a cup of damnation—
Which our Chancellor Comus extols as divine,
To train up our fate and our fortunes—as swine?

Drink, ERIN! drink deep from this crystalline round,
Till the tortures of self-recollection be drown'd;
Till the hopes of thy heart be all stiffen'd to stone—
Then sit down in the dirt, like a queen on her throne.

No frenzy for Freedom to flash o'er the brain;
Thou shalt dance to the musical clank of the chain;
A crown of cheap straw shall seem rich to thine eye,
And peace and good order shall reign in the sty!

Nor boast that no track of the viper is seen,
To stain thy pure surface of Emerald green;
For the Serpent will never want poison to kill,
While the fat of your fields feeds the Worm of the Still!

TO

IRELAND.

My country! shall I mourn, or bless,
Thy tame and wretched happiness?

'Tis true! the vast Atlantic tide
Has scoop'd thy harbours deep, and wide,
Bold to protect, and prompt to save,
From fury of the Western wave:

And Shannon points to Europe's trade,
For THAT, his chain of lakes was made;
For THAT, he scorns to waste his store,
In channel of a subject shore,
But courts the Southern wind to bring
A world, upon its tepid wing.

True! thy resplendent rivers run,
And safe beneath a temp'rate sun
Springs the young verdure of thy plain,
Nor dreads a torrid Eastern reign.

True! thou are blest, in Nature's plan,
Nothing seems wanting here, but—MAN;
Man—to subdue, not serve the soil,
To win, and wear its golden spoil;
Man—conscious of an earth his own,
No savage biped, torpid, prone;
Living, to dog his brother brute,
And hung'ring for a lazy root,
Food for a soft, contented slave;
Not for the hardy and the brave.

Had nature been her enemy,
IERNE might be fierce and free.
To the stout heart, and iron hand,
Temp'rate each sky, and tame each land;
A climate and a soil less kind,
Had formed a map of richer mind.
Now, a mere sterile swamp of SOUL,
Tho' meadows spread, and rivers roll;
A nation of abortive men,
That dart—the tongue; and point—the pen.
And, at the back of Europe, hurl'd—
A base POSTERIOR of the world.

In lap of Araby the blest,
Man lies with luxury opprest;
While spicy odours, blown around,
Enrich the air, and gems—the ground.
But thro' the pathless, burning waste,
Man marches with his patient beast,
Braves the hot sun, and heaving sand,
And calls it free and happy land.

Enough to make a desert known,
" Arms, and the man," and sand and stone!

ASPIRATION.

O! how I long to be at rest!
No more oppressing, or opprest,
To sink asleep, on nature's nursing breast!

In Earth's green cradle to be laid,
Where larks may build, where lambs have play'd,
And a clear stream may flow, and soothe my hov'ring
    shade.

The twilight mem'ry loves to spread,
Haply, may linger o'er my head,
And half illume the long departed dead.

TRANSLATED FROM THE IRISH.

Branch of the sweet excelling rose
That in such pomp of beauty blows,
So passing sweet in smell and sight,
On whom shalt thou bestow delight?

Who, in the dewy evening walk,
Shall pluck thee on thy tender stalk?
Whose temples, blushing, shalt thou twine,
And who inhale thy breath divine?

ON TEA.

EXTRACT.

'Tis at tea that the bud of the lip learns to blow,
That the ice-plant grows gracious, and shakes off the
    snow;
Ev'n him who at dinner, sat mute as a block,
Or like to a lighter that's jamm'd in a lock,
Tea lifts to the level of communication,
And he glides down the current of glib conversation.
Celestial water! true Helicon stream!
Pure fount of the poet's meridian dream—
Divine coalition! tea, sugar, and cream!
Sweet solace of life, from whence happiness springs,
To duchess and dowdy, to cobblers and kings;
It is thine to make body with spirit agree;
Thou art potent to chase e'en the spectre *ennui;*
It is thine the fierce throb of the pulse to restrain,
And raise the sick head from the pallet of pain,
To temper the bitters of family strife,
And slacken, a little, the cordage of life.

EXTRACT.

"Hail! heart-ennobling Solitude
Hail, godlike leisure to be good!
Thee, pensive nun! thy vot'ry hails,
In twilight walks, thro' lonely vales,

Where, melted by the Western breeze,
The moon-beams trickle thro' the trees;
And stillest earth around doth seem
Wrapt as in some golden dream,
And ev'ry ruder thought supprest,
Sooths the calm halcyon of the breast.
Oh! grant me Heav'n, that golden state,
Too low to dread the bolts of fate,
And too ambitious to be great;
Where, shrouded from the glare of folly,
Child of the muse, and melancholy,
I may sink down on nature's breast,
Lull'd by the buzzing world to rest,
And when life fails——
Wrapt in a web of well-spun thought,
By fate-foreboding fancy wrought,
A self-made tomb, like silk-worm lie,
And feel it luxury to die."

ELEGY.

The lonely hours move by with heavy wing,
And April weeps upon the lap of Spring;
Retire, soft month, for cheerful May appears,
Like a fond sister, to dry up thy tears:
Her sunny smile shall chase thy hov'ring show'rs,
Her blushes redden on thy fruits and flow'rs.

I watch the progress of the vernal bloom,
The breath of Spring exhales its sweet perfume;
I feel that ev'ry hope, and ev'ry fear,
Has some new int'rest in the op'ning year;
For ev'ry bud that blows, I think, will bring her here,

Her, whom my heart has made its chosen theme,
My daily visitant, my nightly dream.

Oh! in return, does her soft bosom prove
One partial thought for Edwin, and for Love?
Blest be that thought! oft steal into her mind,
And gently intercede, and woo her to be kind!
Seize some soft moment, that delight employs,
Not such delight as springs from selfish joys,
But such as rather grave than gay appears,
That loves to smile, and sometimes smiles in tears:
When at her touch, soft music breathes around,
When the soul owns its sympathy with sound;
When the heart melts with ev'ry melting tone,
Feels others sorrows, and forgets its own.
Then, blest idea! then suggest the youth,
Whose plea is constancy, whose pride is truth;
In the small circuit of whose scarce-known name,
No pompous pile ascends, no shining spire of fame;
Yet fertile is the soil, and pure the air,
And love has built a modest mansion there;
There folds his wings, forgetful now to roam,
Warms his dear hut and calls it second home;
Wit seldom calls, Pride scorns to be a guest,
And Fashion's flow'rs, but wither on the breast;
But Love is there, a company alone,
And pleads his cause, who fears to plead his own;
Who fears to speak, yet scarcely can conceal,
Whose tongue may falter, but whose heart can feel;
Who cannot boast he ever felt the fire
That burns so fiercely, it must soon expire.
The torch of Love, is form'd of finer flame,
Plac'd in the heart, it sheds its genial beam,
Light of our length'ning life, and glory of our frame.

D

AT A MUSIC MEETING.

O let the soul of Music come,
And call my restless fancy home;
With silken thread of sound, inclose
Her wings, and rock her to repose!

Such whispers of angelic breath,
As quicken spirits chain'd in death;
And gently o'er the senses creep,
And fear to break the sainted sleep!

FROM THE FRENCH.

Cupid, once, of sleep forsaken,
  Pass'd each night in grievous moan;
Doctors came, and drugs were taken,
  The poor child was all but gone.

Hymen call'd, a new physician,
  Sleep that night the eye-lids bless'd;
The next still better'd his condition,
  And soon no boy got sounder rest.

TO
J * * * * C * * * * *,

WHO SAID, "I CARE NOT WHAT THE CROWD MAY THINK."

The crowd, my friend, have common sense,
They feel the pow'r of pounds and pence;

And as they feel, they prize :
For wealth, when rightly understood,
Is the best blessing of the good,
  The wisdom of the wise.

What's wealth ?—Enough, and somewhat over ;
Of this I own myself the lover,
  And who is not's a ninny ;
Of what avail the sun-gilt cot,
Without a pullet in the pot ?
  What's life without a guinea ?

It is to sneak down from a garret,
To sponge on others' beef and claret,
  To get, but not to give ;
To feel each rising wish repress'd,
The wish to be, by blessing blest,
  But this is not to live.

'Tis not to sit, and con a theme,
Or in a smooth pellucid stream,
  The rueful phiz behold ;
And when the lunar light has spread
A yellow radiance o'er thy head,
  To catch poetic gold.

Whate'er the cynic may pretend,
Money, a means, but not an end, ·
  Is happiness below.
Oh ! for a mine of gold to give,
To live, and to make others live,
  And clear the world of woe.

To bless unseen, unseen descend,
On with'ring hearts that want a friend,

Like dew-drops from above;
And oft both seen and felt to pour,
In one abundant Jove-like show'r,
    And fill the lap of Love.

For sharper suff'rings than thy own,
'Tis thine, O Penury, to groan.
    Stretch'd on the rack of life;
Thy cradl'd child unconscious sleeps,
But woe for her who wakes and weeps,
    The mother and the wife.

O Fortune! come and crown my fate,
Wafted along in winning state,
    Like Egypt's Queen of old;
When frequent dash'd the silver oars,
And silken sails perfum'd the shores,
    And Cydnus burn'd with gold.

To youth, and industry, and health,
She comes, the sov'reign good of wealth,
    And ev'ry blessing bears;
But to enjoy her golden mean
It must be felt, it must be seen,
    And save it from your heirs.

———

LINES

TO A YOUNG GENTLEMAN,

AGED SEVENTEEN.

I feel the fragrance of thy early muse,
A modest vi'let, bath'd in morning dews.
Barren the soil, where no such hopes appear,
Blossoms like these, foretel the rip'ning ear.

The harsh preceptor chills with cold disdain,
Kind Nature loves the flow'r before the grain.
In ev'ry age, as ev'ry season kind,
She loves the vernal verdure of the mind;
Smiles on the bud as on the yellow sheaf,
And trains to light and life its soft evolving leaf;
But tho', with wisdom, she can waste her hours.
And fondle with her family of flow'rs,
She hopes to find, as changeful seasons roll,
Fruits more mature, and harvest of the soul;
No off'ring now for her, the poet's pen,
" Flow'rs to the fair," she cries, " but bring me food for
MEN."

IMITATION OF HORACE.

" Exegi monumentum ære perennius." HORACE.

'Tis done—the pyramid of poetry,
In firm magnificence assails the sky;
Fame, on the cloudless top, expands her wings,
And sees below the wasting works of Kings:
For, not one wintry blast so high can climb,
Too deep for sapping show'rs, for tempests too sublime;
And falling snow of years, and noiseless stealth of time.
Beneath that snow, my laurels shall be seen,
In the full freshness of perennial green:
I shall not die, this work, this work shall save
The nobler half of Horace from the grave;
His fame shall 'lighten all succeeding times,
A circling sun around the polar climes,
That dips its disk into the sea of night,
Then mounts again his throne of ever-living light.
For, while the Priest ascends yon pompous road,
Whose long gradation seeks our patron-God,

And, at his side, in sadly pleasing shade,
Moves slow along the mute mysterious maid,
So long my name shall triumph o'er the tomb,
And Horace shall be co-etern with Rome.
Where Upper Nile, in annual phrenzy throws,
The melted mass of Ethiopian snows,
Cleaving the Cliff, that guards Sienna's side
A wild, abrupt, innavigable tide;
There, o'er the cataract, my fame shall soar,
And stoop to hear the repercussive roar.
Where savage Thames, now scarcely known to song,
Winds thro' the Western isle his silv'ry length along,
Pregnant, perhaps, with glories yet to come,
The destin'd Tiber of some greater Rome;
There, shall my verse the sullen climate tame,
And the rich fragrance of Horatian fame
Melt on the tongue, and humanize the heart,
Till barb'rous nature yields to tuneful art.
Horace—who made th' Eolian lyre his own,
To Latin measures harmoniz'd its tone;
While the rack'd strings reveal'd their secret charms,
And Roman arts kept pace with Roman arms.
Assume, my soul! a meritorious state,
And proudly prescient of thy future fate,
Be, what the gods and nature will'd thee—Great.
Come, therefore, come, sublimest of the Nine!
Come forward, from the rest, O! Muse divine,
And with thy facile hand, and with thy smile benign,
Let fall th' eternal laurel on my head,
Adorn me living, and enshrine me dead.

MRS. SIDDONS.

Siddons, accept my tributary tear,
Nor scorn an offering, humble, but sincere;
Not clouds of fragrance curling to the skies,
Nor golden censers form the sacrifice;
More precious far, the hand of humble love,
That on the altar lays " th' unblemish'd dove."

In Thee, the broken heart finds sweet relief,
And lulls its suff'ring with ideal grief;
Lost to the ills of life, it leaves behind
Corroding care, and quarrel of the mind;
The harsh pain softens in thy soothing tone,
Wond'ring, we melt at sorrows not our own;
Our own lie hush'd, in short and balmy sleep,
But 'tis strange happiness, with Thee, to weep.

Blest be that art, which makes misfortune wear
A form so mild, as only costs a tear!
When mirth would madden—can our woes beguile,
When mirth would only force—an agonizing smile.
Delightful, then, to see thy passions roll,
Driv'n in the tempest of Calista's soul.
To mark the wasteful deluge of the breast,
When hov'ring love so vainly seeks to rest;
No light divine, no breath of God to bless,
Wretched, but great, sublime in wickedness!

Ah, SIDDONS! strive not in this dress to win
Our hearts, too facile of themselves to sin;
In thee, the Devil wears something too divine,
And Abra'm's bosom is forgot for thine;

Act from the moral of thy life, and move
With awful dignity of wedded love;
From bold seduction start, and lift thine eyes,
As if to draw the light'ning from the skies;
Then bend at once their fierce collected blaze,
And blast th' astonish'd wretch that kneels and prays.

Let our hearts hear the long-protracted moan,
Pouring its mellow, melancholy tone;
Like the sweet horn that floats upon the gale,
And streams its music down some lonely vale.

Let cares maternal heave the anxious breast,
And clasp thy child, and tremble to be bless'd;
Or, give the look that calms the father's fears,
While the white bosom drinks his falling tears,
Sees the blood redden on his pallid cheek,
And looks a happiness, too great to speak;
Bends o'er his face with eyes of dewy light,
Watches the kindling breath, and smiles supreme delight.

Or, let the poet once allot the part:
Sublime, thy nature, but thy pathos, art.

O! then, assume the port of PALLAS—stand
The stern avenger of a blood-stain'd land,
Beauty and terror mingling in thy face,
With fiery motion, and with awful grace;
O'er the calm eyes, thy curling brows be seen,
Like thunder gath'ring round the blue serene:
Thy black plumes rustle with the coming storm—
WISDOM—to feeble men a fearful form—
On base of adamant thy feet be press'd,
And on thy arm the dreadful Egis rest—
Where endless anguish of the eyes is roll'd,
And round the gasping head the serpents glide in gold,

While life in monumental stone is laid,
As the shield shifts its gloomy breadth of shade—
Then, Goddess, then, move on, with might divine,
The strength and swiftness of thy Sire be thine;
For pow'r Almighty still thro' Wisdom flows,
And blest the bolt of Jove which Pallas throws;
But e'er the vengeance from thy hand be hurl'd,
Stop and address the Giants of the World:—

"Tyrants! for whom lies human life defac'd,
A tangled wilderness, a dreary waste,
Whose savage sport with Nimrod first began.
And down the steeps of time has hunted man;
Made him in ev'ry state, or food, or game,
Pursued him, wild; or kennel'd him, if tame;
Taught human hounds to join the bloody chace,
And fix the famish'd fang in their own wretched race.

"Tyrants! whose arms, upheld by beasts of prey,
Or captive men, more monst'rous still than they;
Lions and tigers, under-propping law,
And grasping charters with contracted paw;
Tyrants! in vain you massacre your kind,
Your swords but serve to propagate—the mind;
Vainly yon pyramid of heads will rise—
My father's eagle from the summit flies,
And seeks some sacred shrine, some Cato's breast,
Where the whole spirit of the pile may rest.
To Cæsar's scale lean'd all the host of heav'n,
Cato, tho' conquer'd, kept the balance even;
The Gods could not destroy the Hero's weight,
Their choice was Fortune, but his will—was Fate.

"Why thus affect the worship of the sky?
Were ye not born?—and are you not to die?

Why make men murmur at the heav'nly pow'rs,
And curse THEIR world because they feel it YOURS?
Because they feel that the same impious plan,
Lifts Men to Gods, and sinks the God to Man—
The God, a piece of ornamented clay—
The Man, a haughty slave, and proud t' obey,
Proud to receive, and proud to give the nod,
To his own morals shapes his docile God;
Yet his hard fate affectedly deplores,
And, the same moment, curses and adores.

"But vain are words, from Wisdom's self addrest,
Terror, alone, can quell the brutal breast;
In this rais'd arm, behold the wrathful flames,
That plunge to Hell your nature and your names,
Endless your sleep—but dreadful be your dreams;
Not the soft sleep, that on the nurse's breast
Smiles in its placid and unruffled rest,
But haunted by despair and fear, behind,
Hurrying with torches thro' the night of mind.

"From torment, Tantalus! for once set free,
Lo! Pitt shall respite thy long misery,
O'er the sweet stream in painful transport hung,
False as his heart, and fluent as his tongue;
Or some fair cloud shall plague his cheated sense,
And tickle still th' eternal impotence.
Colossal Russia shall unpity'd groan,
Raising, in vain, the Sysiphean stone;
At once the mass of nation thunders down,
And grinds to death the murd'ress and her crown.
Prussia! lie stretch'd upon the burning wheel
Of mad ambition and of savage zeal;
Th' imperial Eagle rears his rebel crest,
And turns his vengeance 'gainst the despot's breast;

Shakes the dark wing, and dips the beak in gore,
And Holland croaks along the Stygian shore.

"Down then to Hell, whose stature touch'd the skies,
Because men knelt, and shrunk to pigmy size—
Make thy own Providence, O! Man, and rise!"

———

LOUVET'S HYMN TO DEATH,

TRANSLATED.

Oppressors of my native land!
  In vain have I denounc'd your crimes—
You conquer, and at your command,
  I go, to live in after times.
Freedom! my last farewell receive—
  The tyrant's stroke 'tis base to fly,
Our country lost, the slave MAY live;
  Republicans MUST die.

How base to grasp the golden hire,
  And serve a more than savage zeal;
Better, with dying France, expire;
  Better to brave yon lifted steel.
Freedom! to thee my life I give,
  This steel elicits patriot fire:
Dishonour'd slaves know how to live,
  But Patriots—to expire.

O ye whom great example fires!
  Take arms for liberty and laws:
The player king, with kings conspires;
  Crush Collot—crush their cursed cause.

And you, begot by murder upon fear,
  You trembling tyrant! soon to meet your fall,
Now, quakes your Mountain, O Robespierre!
  And soon shall bury all.

But, ah! possessor of my heart!
  Whom here I see, yet dread to own,
Now, play a more than female part,
  Now, learn to bear distress—alone.
Freedom! shed comfort from above,
  To make her bear the yoke of life;
O spare the quick'ning pledge of love,
  The mother save, if not the wife.

My wife!—as mother, doubly dear,
  With care thy cradled child attend;
And teach, to his attentive ear,
  His Father's glorious end;
To Freedom's altar lead our boy;
  To her high accents, tune his breath;
And let his first, and latest cry,
  Be, "Liberty or Death!"

Should villains in thy time grow great,
  And human blood in torrents flow;
Seek not t' avenge thy Father's fate:
  For France, France, only, strike the blow.
Let future Syllas dread their doom,
  When my young Cato's frown they see;
Or hear him, o'er his Father's tomb,
  Cry, "Give me Death or Liberty!"

Blood-hounds of France! your race is run—
  One Monster welters in his gore;
Angelic Woman here has done
  A deed, which Brutus did before.

O Freedom! lift thy arm sublime,
 Copy the fair Tyrannicide,
Whose virtue rose to balance crime,
 And liv'd—until Marat had died.

I feel the pressing multitude;
 I hear their wild, impatient cry;
How much it costs, to do them good!
 Who lives for them, for them must die.
I go to meet the fond embrace
 Of heroes long to hist'ry known,
And Sydney on this head shall place
 A laurel from his own.

Now take, my eyes, one ling'ring view,
Then bid to France a long adieu!——

WAKE. (³)

1797.

Feminis lugere, honestum est; viris, meminisse.

Here, our brother worthy lies,
Wake not him with women's cries;
Mourn the way that manhood ought;
Sit in silent trance of thought.

Write his merits on your mind,
Morals pure, and manners kind;
In his head, as on a hill,
Virtue plac'd her citadel.

Why cut off in palmy youth?
Truth he spoke, and acted truth;
"Countrymen, Unite!" he cried,
And died, for what his Saviour died!

God of Peace, and God of Love,
Let it not thy vengeance move!
Let it not thy lightnings draw,
A nation guillotin'd by law!

Hapless nation! rent and torn,
Early wert thou taught to mourn!
Warfare of six hundred years!
Epochs mark'd by blood and tears.

Hunted thro' thy native grounds,
A flung reward of human hounds,
Each one pull'd, and tore his share,
Emblem of thy deep despair!

Hapless nation, hapless land:
Heap of uncementing sand!
Crumbled by a foreign weight,
Or by worse, domestic hate!

God of Mercy, God of Peace,
Make the mad confusion cease!
O'er the mental chaos move,
Through it speak the light of love!

Monstrous and unhappy sight!
Brothers' blood will not unite.
Holy oil and holy water,
Mix—and fill the earth with slaughter.

Who is she, with aspect wild ?—
The widow'd Mother, with her child;
Child, new stirring in the womb,
Husband, waiting for the tomb.

Angel of this holy place!
Calm her soul, and whisper, Peace!
Cord, or axe, or guillotine,
Makes the sentence, not the sin.

Here we watch our brother's sleep;
Watch with us, but do not weep:
Watch with us, thro' dead of night—
But expect the morning light.

Conquer Fortune—persevere—
Lo! it breaks—the morning clear!
The cheerful cock awakes the skies;
The day is come—Arise, arise!

LINES

ADDRESSED TO THE AUTHOR OF A LIBEL ON THE PLAYERS. (*)

Thou literary HARLEQUIN!
Whose *mask* brings safety to thy skin,
With patch'd and party-colour'd dress,
Made up of shreds of languages;
A tailor's hell of common-places,
Hoarded for all convenient cases;
Remnants and rags from "hole of glory,"
And lumber of an *attic* story,

The critic's cheap applause to win,
By treasure of an ass's skin.

Thy pocket-mem'ry serves to quote;
Thy wit, enough to point a note;
Thy learning, to make sizers stare;
Thy spirit, to lampoon a play'r.

Resolved to vent satiric spite,
Yet, pre-determined not to fight,
This TEUCER of the pigeon-hole
Seeks a dark place to save his poll,
Then darts his poison'd shafts below,
With little vigour in the bow.

Without one manly, gen'rous aim,
Thine, is an effervescent fame:
Pungent, and volatile, and smart,
Distill'd from vitriol of the heart,
Thy verse throws round its spitter-spatter,
The acid flash of soda-water;
No juice divine, no racy drop,
That flames and mantles in the cup,
And shows the soil from whence it came,
Warm'd with the pure Phœbean beam.

Will the soft wing of flying Time
Drop odour on such stinging rhyme?

O! not for such, the hallow'd bays,
To mem'ry dear, when life decays.
Not such the verse of taste and truth,
The vi'let sweet of primy youth;
Youth, that with flag of hope unfurl'd,
Walks forth, amidst a garden world,

Beholds each blossom of delight,
Fair to the sense, and full in sight,
While pleasure flows from ev'ry part,
And genial nature swells the heart.

Such scenes our youthful bard annoy,
He blights each bursting bud of joy;
The laurel round his temple strays,
To drop its poison, not its praise.
Such venom in the early page,
What will the *virus* be in age?

A sat'rist, in his vernal years,
Like the first foe to man, appears,
When on the tree of life he sate,
And croak'd out Eden's coming fate,
Her blossoms to be tempest-tost,
And Paradise for ever lost.

Trust me, thy marriage with this Muse,
Not long will drop Hyblean dews;
Swiftly must change his honey'd moon,
Who woos and weds the low lampoon;
Swift shall his moon decrease and fall,
Succeeded by a moon of *gall*.
The bile, tho' *splendid*, by degrees
Becomes the cynic's sore disease,
Works to the heart, corrodes unseen,
And makes his breast the cave of spleen;
Till, by a sort of moral trope,
The coxcomb turns a misanthrope;
His ruling maxim, and his fate,
Hated by all, and all to hate.

Where'er he comes, his atmosphere
Turns the sweet smile into a sneer;

E.

The quick and ardent sp'rit of love
Congeals, and can no longer move;
Chill'd to the source of genial heat,
The pulse forgets its mirthful beat,
The flush of pleasure leaves the cheek,
The palsied tongue wants power to speak;
The Graces quit their mazy dance,
And stand, appall'd, in speechless trance:
The voice of music, at its height,
Its airy wheel, and circling flight,
Drops, disconcerted, and distrest,
And sinks into its silent nest:
All Nature dreads the caustic power,
And beauty closes up her flower!

Take, then, in time, the wiser part,
Pluck this ill habit from the heart;
Cast off thy wreath of Aconite,
From cynic, change to parasite;
In velvet sheath conceal thy claws,
And, with soft flatt'ry, purr applause!
Employ thy pen in prittle-prattle,
And still be snake—but drown thy rattle!
For Satire still, with all his cant,
Has more or less of sycophant.

Come forth, and dare the searching Sun,
Nor, like the base assassin, run;
Nor still remain, as now thou'rt seen,
The monster of a Magazine!
So shalt thou rise to worldly fame,
And borrow a sublimer name
Than now you share with Johnson's wife,
A POISONER of the BREAD of LIFE.

JUVENAL.

EIGHTH SATIRE.

"Stemmata quid faciant."

Say, ye who perch on lofty pedigree,
What fruit is gather'd from the parchment tree?
Broad as it spreads, and tow'ring to the skies,
From root plebeian its first glories rise;
What then avails, when rightly understood,
The boast of ancestry, the pride of blood?
Through the long gall'ries pictur'd walk to tread,
And, pompous, ponder on the mighty dead,
Where greatness rattles in some rotten frame,
And the moth feeds on beauty's fading flame.
O'er the pale portrait, and the noseless bust,
Oblivion strews a soft sepulchral dust;
The line illustrious seems to stain the wall,
And one sublime of soot envelopes all.

What could the trophied lye to Howe atone
For British honour mortgag'd with his own?
His nightly cares and watchings, to sustain
A bank at pharo, and a chess-campaign?
While Wolfe, on high, in pictur'd glory, lies,
The cry of "vict'ry!" hails, and, smiling, dies!
Dare Courtenay claim the honours of his kind?
The pompous lineage shames the pigmy mind.
His coat armorial, chalk'd upon the floor,
Costs what would satiate a thousand poor;
Well pleas'd the Peer, one moment to amuse,
Then yields the pageant to the dancer's shoes.

Base born such men, though fill'd with regal blood,
The truly noble are the truly good;

And he whose morals through his manners shine,
May boast himself of the Milesian line.
Let plain humility precede his Grace,
Let modest merit walk before the mace:
Office and rank are duties of the mind,
The rights they claim, are debts they owe mankind;
And not a voice among the nameless crowd,
That may not cry, " 'Tis I who make them proud."

    To rule strong passions with a calm control,
To spread around a sanctity of soul,
That meets, serene, the fame of public strife,
And perfumes every act of lesser life;
Virtue to feel, and virtue to impart,
That household God which consecrates the heart,
Flies from the fretted roof, the gilded dome,
To rest within an humbler, happier home;
Behold the GENTLEMAN—confess'd and clear,
For Nature's patent never made a Peer,
The mean ennobled, nor adorn'd the base;
Merit alone, with her creates a race.

    Conspicuous stars, in chart of hist'ry plac'd,
To cheer the dreary biographic waste,
In their own right, they take their seats sublime,
And break illustrious through the cloud of time.

    From nicknam'd curs these titles first began—
A Spaniel, Cato—then my Lord, a Man.
The self-same irony was fram'd to suit
The fawning biped, and the fawning brute;
While Pompey snores upon my Lady's lap,
The infant Lordling feeds, or starves, on pap.
Puppies well-bred, are Cæsar'd into fame,
And TOMMY TOWNSEND takes great SIDNEY'S name.

Still as the name grows soil'd, and gathers dirt,
They shift their title, as they change their shirt ;
Some newer honour makes them white and fair,
SIDNEY soaps TOM, and JACK is cleans'd by CLARE !
But how could wash of heraldry efface
The name of BURKE, and dignify disgrace !
Could peerage blazon o'er the pension'd page,
Or give a gloss to ignominious age !
Himself the prime corrupter of his laws,
Himself, the grievance which incens'd he draws ;
Not to be blam'd but in a tender tone,
Not to be prais'd, but with a heart-felt groan.
He lives a lesson for all future time,
Pathetically great, and painfully sublime.

O ! why is genius curs'd with length of days ?
The head still flourishing, the heart decays ;
Protracted life makes virtue less secure,
The death of wits is seldom premature.

Quench'd too by years, gigantic JOHNSON's zeal,
The unwieldly elephant was taught to kneel ;
Bore his strong tower to please a servile court,
And wreathed his lithe proboscis for their sport.

Return to him, from whom our Satire springs,
Rich in the blood of concubines and kings.
"Avaunt !" he cries, " ye vulgar and ye base,
Learn the prerogatives of royal race ;
From YORK and LANCASTER, conjoin'd, I come,
Sink down, ye dregs, I float at top—the scum !"

Yet grant that some, the lowest of the throng,
Have known the right, as well as felt the wrong ;
That he who rul'd, with iron rod, the skies,
And at whose feet the broken sceptre lies ;

Grant, that such men, the Adams of their line,
Spring from the earth, but own a sire divine;
While you, with ancestry around you plac'd,
In bronze or marble, porcelain or paste;
May rise at death, to alabaster fame,
And gain the smoke of honour, not the flame.

In all so high in rank, or man, or woman;
No sense so rare, as what we call the common.
Scorning the level, they ascend the skies,
Like the puff'd bag, whose lightness makes it rise;
Titles and arms the varnish'd silk may bear,
Within—'tis nought but pestilential air.

What's honour?—Virtue to its height refin'd,
The felt aroma of the unseen mind,
That cheers the senses, tho' it cheats the sight,
And spreads abroad its elegant delight.
Turn from the past, and bring thy honours home—
Thyself the ancestor, for times to come.
Not the low parasite who prowls for bread,
So mean as he who lives upon the dead,
From some dried mummy draws his noble claim,
Snuffs up the fœtor, and believes it fame.

Be just, be generous, self-dependent, brave;
Think nothing meaner than a titled slave;
Coolly resolved to act the patriot part,
Join SIDNEY's pulse to RUSSELL's generous heart:
With proud complacence stand, like PALMER, pure,
Or, with mild dignity of honest MUIR,
Before the brazen bulls of law, and hear
The savage sentence, with a smile severe;
A smile that deems it mercy to be hurl'd,
Where one may tread against the present world.*

* Allusion to the Antipodes.

What is life, here—its zest and spirit gone,
The flower faded, and its essence flown?
What precious balm, what aromatic art,
Can cleanse pollution from the public heart?

Better to make the farthest earth our home,
With Nature's commoners at large to roam,
Than join this social war of clan to clan,
Where civil life has barbariz'd the man.

Here, meet th' extremes of rank : here, social art
Has levell'd mankind by the selfish heart.
Here, no contented middle rank we trace,
The sole ambition—to be rich and base.
Some, o'er their native element, elate,
Like ice-form'd islands, tow'r in frozen state ;
Repel all nature with their gelid breath,
And what seems harbour, is the jaw of death ;
The wretched mass beat down the struggling mind—
Nor see, nor feel their country, nor their kind ;
But bow the back, and bend the eye to earth,
And strangle feeling in its infant birth ;
Through all, extends one sterile swamp of soul,
And fogs of apathy invest the whole.

Thrice blest in fate, had STRONGBOW never bore
His band of robbers to green ERIN's shore !
In savage times, the seat of learning known,
In times refin'd, itself the savage grown ;
Left to herself, she of herself had join'd
Surrounding nations, in the race of mind,
With them, work'd off the rough barbarian soul,
With them, progressive to a common goal.
Her petty chieftains, conquered by the throne,
For common interest, while it meant its own ;

By law, at length, the King to people chain'd,
His duties modell'd, and their rights maintain'd,
From strong collision of internal strife,
Had sprung an energy of public life,
(For pain and travail that precede the birth,
Endear sweet freedom to the mother earth,)
Then man had rais'd his spacious forehead high,
Lord of himself, the sea, the soil, the sky;
Twin'd round his sword the wreath of civic art,
And prov'd the wisdom of a fearless heart:
No penal code had then impal'd the land—
No stranger Court, no King at second hand.

TO

SARAH DRENNAN,

WITH A RING.

Emblem of happiness, not bought, nor sold,
Accept this modest RING of virgin gold.
Love, in the small but perfect circle, trace,
And duty in its soft, tho' strict embrace.
Plain, precious, pure, as best becomes the wife;
Yet firm to bear the frequent rubs of life.
Connubial life disdains a fragile toy,
Which rust can tarnish, or a touch destroy,
Nor much admires, what courts the gen'ral gaze,
The dazzling diamond's meretricious blaze,
That hides, with glare, the anguish of a heart
By nature hard, tho' polish'd bright—by art.
More to my taste, the ornament that shows
Domestic bliss, and, without glaring, glows.

Whose gentle pressure serves to keep the mind
To all correct, to one discreetly kind.
Of simple elegance, th' unconscious charm—
The holy amulet to keep from harm;
To guard at once and consecrate the shrine,
Take this dear pledge, it makes, and keeps thee—MINE.

————

TO

HIS WIFE.

WITH A BRANCH OF SWEET-BRIAR.

How sweet, how short is beauty's power!
   A passing, partial grace,
In bud, in blossom, and in flow'r,
   In female form or face!

But when the flow'r pervades the tree,
   The likeness is complete,
Between *this* fragrant shrub and thee—
   For *every* leaf is sweet.

————

RELIGIOUS POEMS.

I.

O thou, who, from thy Heav'n of Love,
   To man in mercy came,
And took, descending from above,
   His nature and his name;

HUMANITY, thou sent of God,
  When earth was heard to mourn,
To trace the steps our Saviour trod,
  And wait till his return!

Here, Angel Virtue! shake thy plumes;
  Their incense here impart;
And wing the willing hand, that comes
  With succour from the heart.

FAITH, at thy side, shall close attend,
  And point her golden rod;
While HOPE, still bright'ning to the end,
  Here seeks her parent God.

O God! may these three graces bind
  In one resplendent zone,
The destinies of human-kind,
  And hang them to thy throne.

II.

Why does the will of Heav'n ordain
  A world so mix'd with woe?
Why pour down want, disease, and pain,
  On wretched man below?

It was the will of God to leave
  These ills for man to mend,
Nor let affliction pass the grave,
  Before it found a friend.

It was by sympathetic ties
  The human race to bind;
To warm the heart, and fill the eyes,
  With pity for our kind.

Pity, that, like the heav'nly bow,
  On darkest cloud doth shine,
And makes, with a celestial glow,
  The human face divine.

Where Mercy takes her 'custom'd stand,
  To bid her flock rejoice,
'Tis there, with grace extends the hand,
  There, Music tunes the voice.

And he who speaks in Mercy's name,
  No fiction needs, nor art;
The still, small voice of Nature's claim,
  Re-echoes through each heart.

Where Pity's frequent tear is shed,
  There God is seen, is found;
Descends upon the hallow'd head,
  And sheds a glory round.

But Charity itself may fail,
  Which doth not active prove;
Nor will the prayer of Faith avail,
  Without the works of Love.

III.

All Nature feels attractive pow'r,
  A strong embracing force;
The drops that sparkle in the show'r,
  The planets in their course.

Thus, in the universe of mind,
  Is felt the law of love,
The charity, both strong and kind,
  For all that live and move.

In this fine sympathetic chain,
  All creatures bear a part;
Their ev'ry pleasure, ev'ry pain,
  Link'd to the feeling heart.

More perfect bond, the Christian plan
  Attaches soul to soul;
Our neighbour is the suffering man,
  Though at the farthest pole.

To earth below, from Heav'n above,
  The faith in Christ profess'd,
More clear reveals that God is Love,
  And whom he loves is blest.

Lo! how the Sun, at glorious dawn,
  The whole horizon fills,
When, all the starry host withdrawn,
  He mounts the Eastern hills!

IV.

O sweeter than the fragrant flow'r,
  At ev'ning's dewy close,
The will, united with the pow'r,
  To succour human woes!

And softer than the softest strain
  Of music to the ear,
The placid joy we give and gain,
  By gratitude sincere.

The husbandman goes forth a-field,
  What hopes his heart expand!
What calm delight his labours yield!
  A harvest—from his hand!

A hand that providently throws,
  Not dissipates in vain;
How neat his field! how clean it grows!
  What produce from each grain!

The nobler husbandry of mind,
  And culture of the heart,—
Shall this, with men, less favour find,
  Less genuine joy impart?

O! no—your goodness strikes a root
  That dies not, nor decays,
And future life shall yield the fruit,
  Which blossoms now in praise.

The youthful hopes, that now expand
  Their green and tender leaves,
Shall spread a plenty o'er the land,
  In rich and yellow sheaves.

Thus, a small bounty well bestow'd,
  May perfect Heaven's high plan;
First daughter to the love of God.
  Is Charity to Man.

'Tis he, who scatters blessings round,
  Adores his Maker best;
His walk through life is mercy-crown'd,
  His bed of death is blest.

V.

The Heav'n of Heav'ns cannot contain
  The Universal Lord;
Yet He, in humble hearts, will deign
  To dwell, and be ador'd.

Where'er ascends the sacrifice
  Of fervent praise and pray'r,
Or on the earth, or in the skies,
  The Heav'n of God is there.

His presence there is spread abroad,
  Through realms, through worlds unknown:
Who seeks the mercies of his God,
  Is ever near his throne.

VI.

In this fair globe, with ocean bound,
And with the starry concave crown'd,
In earth below, in Heav'n above,
How clear reveal'd, that God is Love!

I seem to hear th' angelic voice,
  Which bless'd the work, and bade, "Rejoice!"
It vibrates still from ev'ry part,
And echoes through my grateful heart.

In God all creatures live and move,
"Motes in the sun-beam of his love;"
Vast Nature quickens in his sight,
Existence feels, and new delight.

Thro' glad creation's ample range
Rolls on the wheel of ceaseless change:
The Phœnix renovates his breath,
Nor dreads destruction, ev'n in death.

From ashes of this world, sublime
Beyond the reach of thought or time,
On wings of faith and hope he soars,
And "Truth in Love" eternally adores.

MY FATHER.

Who took me from my mother's arms,
And, smiling at her soft alarms,
Show'd me the world, and nature's charms?
                MY FATHER!

Who made me feel, and understand,
The wonders of the sea and land,
And mark, through all, the Makers hand?

Who climb'd with me the mountain's height,
And watch'd my look of dread delight,
While rose the glorious orb of light?

Who from each flow'r and verdant stalk,
Gather'd a honey'd store of talk,
And fill'd the long delightful walk?

Not on an insect would he tread,
Nor strike the stinging nettle dead,
Who taught, at once, my heart and head—

Who fir'd my breast with Homer's fame,
And taught the high, heroic theme,
That nightly flashed upon my dream?

Who smiled at my supreme desire
To see the curling smoke aspire,
From Ithaca's domestic fire?

Who, with Ulysses, saw me roam,
High on the raft, amidst the foam,
His head uprais'd to look for home?

"What made a barren rock so dear?"
"My boy, he had a country there!"
And who, then, dropt a prescient tear?

Who now, in pale and placid light
Of mem'ry, gleams upon my sight,
Bursting the sepulchre of night?

O! teach me still thy Christian plan,
For practice with thy precept ran,
Nor yet desert me, now a man—

Still let thy scholar's heart rejoice,
With charm of thy angelic voice;
Still prompt the motive and the choice—

For yet remains a little space,
Till I shall meet the face to face,
And not (as now) in vain embrace,

MY FATHER!

EPITAPH

ON

M. D.

BORN JUNE 3RD, DIED SEPT. 16, 1803.

Short was thy day, sweet babe! but this will give
A longer space of Heav'nly life to live.
Yet, with delight, you drew your balmy breath,
And the first pain you seem'd to feel, was—death.
Nor death itself could violate thy face,
Its pleas'd expression, and its placid grace.
I now commit thee to a mother's breast,
Where thou shalt sleep, and wake—to be more blest;
New beams of meaning kindle in thine eyes,
And a new world excite their glad surprise.
Soon, by your side, shall rise a rustic tomb,
And the turf heave, to give a parent room.
Enough, to consecrate this humbler bier,
Thy infant innocence—*his* gushing tear.

W. D.

1806. AGED 50.

And now, with a pencil impartial, though kind,
Let me picture myself, from the mirror of mind.

What a deep tint of gravity saddens that face!
A smile evanescent, a lightening grace,
Endeavours by fits, but in vain, to illume,
And more clearly reveals constitutional gloom.

Yet, to confidence open, and cordial, and bland,
In this gay burst of sunshine, his feelings expand;
But once chill'd by distrust, he then scorns to explain,
Nor a doubt to disperse, would a sentiment feign.

Most social, alone; but alone in the crowd,
With candour, reserved, and with diffidence, proud;
His manners so cold, so repulsive, so shy,
One might think that the fountain of feeling was dry;
Yet his nature was soft—situation alone
Can make petrified water seem absolute stone;
But no sooner is felt the elective attraction,
Than it quick re-dissolves into tears of affection.

Man of taste, more than talent; not learn'd, tho' of
    letters;
His creed without claws, and his faith without fetters;
But full plum'd with hope and with charity, soars,
Or, mutely expectant, confides, and adores.

Still shrinking from praise, tho' in search of a name,
He trod on the brink of precipitate fame;
And stretch'd forth his arm to the beckoning form,
A vision of glory, which flash'd thro' the storm;
INDEPENDENCE shot past him in letters of light,
Then the scroll seem'd to shrivel, and vanish in night;
And all the illumin'd horizon became,
In the shift of the moment, a darkness—a dream.

The world he knew well, yet he felt some disdain
To turn such a knowledge to traffic and gain;
The GENTLEMAN scrupled to call to his aid
The craft of a calling, and tricks of a trade.
To live on the public, and live at your ease,
To retain independence, yet pocket the fees,

Is a problem, which, tho' he threw down in despair,
May prove easy to him who the circle can square.

No lithe interloper, no courteous encroacher,
No practice detailer, no puffer, no poacher,
He valued too lightly the skill he possèss'd,
But the world seem'd to think he must know himself
    best.
Thus ling'ring thro' life, 'tween profession and will,
The most lib'ral of arts seem'd a livery still;
    Then, he long'd, (how he long'd!) to obtain his dis-
        discharge;
And walk forth a gentleman, free and at large.
(Romantic disclaimer of patient and pelf,)
A king o'er ten acres, a sovereign of self.

In a classical cot, that retires to be seen,
Of a clear cheerful white, deep embosom'd in green,
Where not a mere taste doth embellish the ground,
But a certain morality breathes all around,
And seems to unite, in diminutive plan,
The graces of nature, and merit of man;
As to picture its owner the spot was design'd,
Not his hand, not his purse—but his feelings, his mind;
The order, the neatness, the quiet, impress'd
On the scen'ry around, which now reign in his breast.

O'er his wide garden-world, sole dictator to stand,
And no landlord to own, but the Lord of all land;
While his trees seem to triumph in sentiment too,
And wave to the town an indignant adieu!

With his boys at his knees, and with HER at his side,
For six years his wife, and the same years his bride;

Thro' the months of these years not one moon made of
    gall,
Her good-nature and cheerfulness honey'd them all ;
And with HER, who, in conduct and counsel doth blend
The Sister, the Parent, Minerva, and Friend,
Through a circle of years, (both their bright and dark
    days,)
His best inspiration, his trust, and his praise :
And with HER, who through life has so quietly mov'd,
So secretly fear'd, and so silently lov'd.
Thus to sit, fancy-crown'd, in an arbour of ease,
While his boys, like his blossoms, drink health from the
    breeze,
Their cheeks rosy-red with ingenuous shame,
A colour most priz'd by the high Spartan dame.

    No pale academics, of classical art,
With pert premature head, and cold cucumber heart ;
But evolv'd by degrees, while they brighten in bloom;
And affection exhales its enchanting perfume.
The home-bred attachment most deeply impress'd,
Will make Country's bare name beat a drum in the
    breast ;
Early prejudice plants what of ripe reason will prove,
And authority binds by the kisses of love ;
Till Duty will feel it her dearest delight,
To speak all the truth, and to act all the right.

This—this is to save what of life we can save,
And the heart of the parent shall pant in the grave !

    Thus, enough in the world to know well for whom
    made,
And enough in the sun, just to shine in the shade ;
Enough, too, of life, when in children renew'd,
Its estimate made, and its end understood,

As survey'd from the summit of full fifty years,
It meander'd along thro' its hopes and its fears;
Till at last it expands in a lake's placid breast,
Where the image of Heaven seems willing to rest;
A mirror of life, and a moral, it shows,
As serenely it heaves in its hallow'd repose.

THOMAS DRENNAN.

DIED ANNO ÆT., 12.

The Spring returns,—but not to thee, sweet boy,
  Glides o'er thy grave her animating breath;
Nature awakes to light, and life, and joy!
  —No vernal warmth can pierce the bed of death.

Beside thee, blush'd, upon the winter snows,
  Charming the eyes, nor dreading swift decline,
At Spring's return then died, the kindred ROSE,
  As if its tender life were knit with thine.

Clos'd the fair promise of thy op'ning year,
  Thy early blossoms, thy affections kind;
Soft smiles evolving from the heart sincere,
  And sweet developement of beauteous mind.

A mind, by manners, more than words, express'd;
  Social, yet secret; resolute, tho' mild;
Truth set her seal upon his candid breast,
  And character was stampt, while yet a child

I saw my father pictur'd in my son;
His life, I hop'd, would glide as smooth away;
And when the calm, sequester'd course was run,
The morn and eve, might make one sabbath day.

Placid, benign, contemplative, and pure,
Such was my father, such wert thou, my child!
Thy flow'r, I hop'd, would bear *his* fruit mature,
Thy happy morn attain his ev'ning mild.

But vain, for thee, these hopes to Heav'n exhal'd,
Tho' watch'd, beside, with twice maternal care;
Nor force of nature, skill of art avail'd,
Nor stranger's blessing, nor the poor man's pray'r.

As from the small, remotest star, descends
The momentary speed of light divine,
Th' angelic nature, thus, with mortal, blends,
And, thus, thy spirit, may converse with mine.

Where lov'd in life, and humanly ador'd,
Here, let thy presence shed a sainted grace;
Thy courteous form to these known walks restor'd
Be its good Genius still, and sanctify the place!

Cabin-Hill, 1812.

ALCAIC ODE BY GRAY,

ATTEMPTED IN ENGLISH.

" Magnis tamen excidit ausis."

Thou, yet unnamed, but whose conspicuous face,
Revealed in features of terrific grace,
Shines, a religion, to this savage place!

In gloom of groves, in gush of fountains clear,
Thy dread divinity approaches near,
Taming the human heart by blended love and fear.

Not beneath domes, that arch their mimic skies,
Peopled with bronze and marble deities,
Canova's wonder-working hand supplies :

But 'midst these rocks, precipitous and rude,
And cliffs, deep cloven by the thundering flood,
And caverns, shrouded with a night of wood :

Here dwells the God, to vulgar minds unknown ;
And now, descending from yon craggy throne,
He makes the temple of the mind his own.

Here let me wait, beside these sacred springs,
List'ning the wafture of angelic wings,
And drink oblivion of all mortal things.

Yet, should stern fortune keep the sigh supprest,
Forced to forsake this silent, secret nest,
Through toils and dangers, lab'ring to be blest—

If the pursuits of pleasure, pow'r, or gain,
(Shrewd in the means, but in their end insane,)
Absorb me in that whirlpool world again ;

At least, good angel, spare my sinking age,
When disappointment has confirmed me sage,
One hallowed nook in this wild hermitage !

Escaped from men, their tumults, crimes, and woes.
Life, like sweet music, breathes a dying close,
Then let me, let me steal to more profound repose !

LINES

WRITTEN IN A COPY OF ROBINSON CRUSOE.

Mark, in this book, th' inventive powers of man;
In worst extremes, what resolution can;
How the soul, kindling in the glorious strife,
Compels a good from every ill of life;
Outlives the storm, the sea-worn wreck explores,
Mans the rich raft, and gains the savage shores:
There builds, there plants, there stores the grain, the fruit,
Talks with the parrot, educates the brute;
Cheers the lone desert with the mimic voice,
And bids its wond'ring echoes cry, rejoice!
Thus, in the world, and in the wilderness,
Strong to create, and provident to bless,
Man finds, or makes, his share of happiness.
And thus, in Crusoe, has there been designed
A chart of life to serve for all his kind!
Even THOU, great exile from the Gallic throne,
Sublimest spectacle in hist'ry shown,
From a poor sailor's fate, may bear and bless thy own!
The art to kill, let other heroes give,
Now, learn to live, and to let others live!

IN THE POSTHUMOUS VOLUME OF
COWPER'S WORKS.

Cowper! were Palestine thy place of birth,
When CHRIST arose on a benighted earth,
The loved disciple, chosen from the rest,
Thou would'st have leaned upon the Saviour's breast;

And the same word which bade the tempest cease,
To thee, poor sinless suff'rer, whispered peace!

THE HARP.

The Harp, our glory once, but now our shame,
Follow'd my Country's fate, and slept without a name.
Angelic ERIN brush'd it with her wings—
Surpris'd by sudden life, the trembling strings
Faintly gave forth one recollective strain,
Then sought the quiet of the Tomb again!

VERSES

BY

JOHN S. DRENNAN, M.D.

VERSES

BY

J. S. DRENNAN, M.D.

FALSE DERMOD.

Cloaked like crime the moon is flying,
  Like revenge the billows roar,
Moans the blast like victim dying,
  Round that lonely shore.
'Neath yon crag, like wizard kneeling,
  Lies a boat with shattered bow,
For no light is in the shieling
  On the headland now!

Many a night a slender taper
  Wooed from thence false Dermod's sight,
Led him through the tempest-vapour
  Safely, many a night.

Quenched that beacon's wistful burning,
  Cold the hand that did prepare,
Dermod's eyes now slowly turning
  Meet but darkness there.

Yet when angry Heaven's designing,
  Here his blood-stained bark destroyed,
Was there not a sudden shining
  In yon chamber void?
Is it guilt-stung Fancy's throbbing,
  Or a voice that thence doth flee,
Sighing 'gainst the wind, and sobbing,
  Sobbing toward the sea?

Lo! by yonder nighmost cape,
  Where the waves are louder knelling,
What is glimmering into shape?
Can the drowned, the dead escape?
  "God of mercy—Ellen!"

"Blows—availed they not to stun her!
  Was the knife deceptive!
Sprang the anchor loose to shun her!
All the black waves piled upon her,
  Shrank they from their captive!"

Pale she stands, as death had crowned her,
  'Mid the waters seething;
Fixed she stands as fate had bound her,
And the wail that gurgles round her
  Is not of *her* breathing.

Round her, through her, like despair,
  Writhes the ocean eddy;
But she does not move—her hair
Sways not in the whirling air,
  And her glance—how steady!

O, that look once seen before!
  O, that gaze undying!
Him, the trembler on the shore,
She is eyeing—nothing more—
  Only coldly eyeing!

"O, the fell, the fiendish deed,
  Vainly wrought to sever,
Is this, is this its maddening meed,
To see her rise again, and bleed
  For ever thus, for ever!"

Coldly, coldly, as before,
  Stands she unreplying.
Him, the traitor on the shore,
Eyeing coldly—nothing more—
  Only coldly eyeing!

"Has the night no cloud to hide
  That still spectre's pleading!
Will not storm, or driving tide,
Force that pointing hand aside!
  Staunch that bosom's bleeding!"

Louder swells the tempest's roar,
  Wilder waves are flying,
But the murdered, as before,
Him, the murderer on the shore,
  Still is eyeing, eyeing!

Thus, as through the shrieking air,
  Streams that light unwonted,
Thus the long night stand they there,
Spectre's glance with murderer's glare
  Terribly confronted!

But when o'er the upland waste
  Morning glimmers red,
Moves the phantom, and aghast,
Seaward pointing as it passed,
  Falls its watcher dead!

DREAMS

Ye Meteors of the Mind that rise
  When Reason's lucid task is done,
Like the night-sheen of polar skies
  That simulates the sun.

Ye Dreams! in whose fictitious sphere,
  To him that guards the mouldering urn,
The Dead, unquestioned by a tear,
  The Lost, of right, return;

Where round the couch of dying men
  Flushed childhood gambols as of yore,
And timeless Beauty smiles again,
  True as she smiled before!

In what quaint labyrinthine caves,
  By what fantastic stems or streams,
Upon the hills, beside the waves,
  Have ye your dwelling, Dreams.

Whence gliding through th' unconscious air,
  As sun and stars successive roll,
Shake ye the lion in his lair?
  Thrill ye the human soul?

Now breathing soft a lenient spell,
　Fleet ministers of grace ye roam,
Bearing the captive from his cell,
　The outcast to his home.

Anon on Furies' wings ye fly,
　Where sceptred crime hath stained the land,
And with inexorable eye
　Palsy the regal hand.

In what dim "interlunar caves,"
　By what abrupt abysmal streams,
Beyond the clouds, below the waves,
　Weave ye your magic, Dreams?

The camp, the cloister, and the mart,
　Are mirrored on your tablets thin,
And oft for the foreboding heart,
　The Future, there, shines in.

The storm-doomed sailor's bride afar
　Shrieks o'er the surges of her sleep;
Upstarting from the visioned war
　Its destined orphans weep.

Oft, too, by pilgrim passion sought,
　As parched he wends his desert way,
Along the glimmering verge of thought,
　Your mimic fountains play!

To what profound prophetic caves,
　O'er what vague-whispering woods or streams,
As Fear evokes, or Fancy raves,
　Shifts your dominion, Dreams?

A WAIL,

1847.

Lament for the land where the sun-beams wander,
   Amid shadows deeper than elsewhere fall,
And the listless winds seem to wail and ponder
   Over glories past which they can't recal.
Fair are its cities, but despair frequents them,
   From its fertile valleys must the famished flee ;
And coasts safe smiling where the wave indents them
   Invite, Isle of Ruin, no hope to thee !
           Ochone for thee, Erin, ochone, a ree !

Round thy mystic towers and cromlechs lonely
   Flit shadows majestic, of chief and sage,
But the light on each clarsech and torque is only
   Dimly reflected to this darkened age.
Felled are thy tall trees that erst branched so boldly,
   Hushed thy sweet singers that once warbled free ;
O the bleak fortune that now clasps thee coldly,
   When, Isle of Ruin, shall it pass from thee ?
           Ochone for thee, Erin, &c.

It has reached the Dead in thy green raths lying,
   'Tis troubling the calm of thy stone-girt rest,
Till a dreary sound of sepulchral sighing
   Echoes the groans of the living breast.
From the Cairns of Meath to grey Cashel's Station
   Dim hands are shudd'ring from sea to sea,
Through Ceim-an-each's Pass floats thy knell,
   lost nation,
   And o'er Glendalloch spirits 'keen' for thee ;
           Ochone for thee, Erin, &c.

THE PECULIAR MAN.

" Rara avis in terris."

I knew a man—I think I knew
  His mind no less than outward feature,
Though there were corners not a few
  And curious crypts within his nature,
Still was he on deliberate view
  Quite an intelligible creature,
Howe'er "Hoi polloi," captious clan
Had dubbed him a " peculiar man."

Peculiar was he in the sense
  He did not just as did his neighbour,
Rated not pleasure by expense,
  Nor meted loveliness by labour;
Some minds would seem to have corns, and hence,
  Don't dance to others' pipe and tabor,
And such non-saltatory plan,
Was that of this " peculiar man."

On state affairs, their links and springs,
  He dogmatised to small extent,
Was not quite hand and glove with kings,
  Nor always knew what patriots meant,
No turn or tendency of things
  Gave him assurance of th' event;
" Who shall the flirts of Fortune's fan
Constrain?" asked " the peculiar man."

Ne'er shone religion to his sight
  In theologic dust and rumpus,
Whilst loftiest pulpit dwindled quite,
  By blatant bigot used a "stump" as;
He could not points of faith unite
  With points of dress, or of the compass,
So some inferred he worshipped Pan,
The dreadfully peculiar man!

He went not gipseying after science,
  Nor made her one with witchcraft nearly,
In German quacks had no affiance,
  And held, "Clairvoyantes" don't see clearly;
There too were literary lions,
  By him accounted poodles merely,
And when they roared from stage or van,
"Bow wow," said the "peculiar man."

In "testimonials," neat or fine,
  Small capital he e'er invested,
And aidless let the Virtues shine,
  On tea-pot "chaste" or tankard crested.
Addresses he was slow to sign,
  And public dinners ill digested;
In short, he had put under ban
"Blarney"—this most "peculiar man."

Blarney ne'er fibbed or fobbed the less,
  "Growl on," grinned she, "O thriftless blockhead!"
"To cant—to cringe, with 'push,' address,
  And honor—to the breeches' pocket,
These 'open sesames' of success,
  Are mine though Right and Reason lock it,
And wit repel, with keener than
Your weapons, my 'peculiar man.'"

Never had nymph's distracting eyes
  Set him the fullest moon invoking;
He held no "shares" of *any* size,
  Nor always of the crops was croaking:
Last in his list of oddities,
  He shaved himself and hated smoking!
'Twould need, I fear, a spick-and-span
New world for such "peculiar man."

He died one day—*that* was not odd;
  Died, but eschewed the undertaker;
And deprecating human laud,
  His memory trembled to his maker.
His sepulchre a nameless sod,
  Dim forests round it many an acre,
With wish fulfilled no eye should scan
That grave—sleeps the "peculiar man."

ON THE TELESCOPIC MOON.

A lifeless solitude—an angry waste,
Scaring our alien eyes with horrors bare;
No fertilizing cloud—no genial air
To mitigate its savageness of breast;
The light itself all undiffusive there;
Motionless terror clinging to the crest
Of steepmost pinnacles; as by despair
Unfathomable caverns still possessed!
How shall we designate such world forlorn?
What nook of Heaven abhors this portent dark?
Lo! where the *Moon* reveals her gentle ray,
Waking the nightingale's and poet's lay;
Speeding benign the voyager's return;
And lighting furtive kisses to their mark!

ON THE SAME.

Bless us, is this the Moon! Is this indeed,
 Messrs. the Poets, *your* particular planet!
 Rough as a porcupine, and bare as granite.
Is this the delicate Dian of your creed!
Cynthia and Phœbe, beauties of this breed!
 Cars, pinnaces (O lud, to mount or man it!)
 Bows, shields, lamps, sick ones, reaping hooks, just
  scan it,
And witness how your similies succeed!
Strong is my faith, ye minstrels, and consoling,
 That once your eyes are steadied to explore
  The Moon's true phiz with clear and specular ken,
In their fine frenzies they'll give over rolling
 In *that* direction, and your tongues no more
  Babble about her, lunatic gentlemen.

PERDITA.

From the dusk forest or the darkening strand,
 Why dost thou come,
Trembling and chill, as if a spectre's hand
 Had warned thee home?
Oft hast thou lingered on the hills afar,
 And roamed the heath,
To win, thou saidst, the lustre of the star,
 The night-flower's breath:
Oft hast thou loosed upon the twilight shore
 Thy lonely sail,
But ne'er returning met my kiss before,
 Thus still and pale.

Hath some deceptive planet mocked thy vow
    With sudden blight?
Yes, mother, I *have* felt upon my brow
    Disastrous light!
Or didst thou in the tangled forest grass
    A serpent wake,
With venom 'neath his shining folds? Alas,
    It *was* a snake!
Haply some bright-eyed vampire that hath crept
    Thy sleep upon,
Thus hueless left thy cheek? 'twas so, she wept,
    'Twas such an one!
Or, is it the beguilement that thus mute
    Thou seek'st to smother,
Of treach'rous berry, or false rinded fruit?
    'Tis poison, Mother.
Such feigned mishap, such heedless enterprise,
    Might well befal;
But I can read in those averted eyes
    A worse than all;
Maiden, is *Love* the cause of thy despair?
    She bowed her head,
Shook down the shining shadow of her hair,
    And nothing said.

THE FIRST FALL OF SNOW.

The Poet gave up his disconsolate task,
For his ink and his blood seemed alike to be freezing;
And to quicken his pulse without fagot or flask,
    Fell to coughing and wheezing.

December had come, and 'twas cold as the tomb ;
'Twas midnight, and Earth lay dark-crouching below,
When something swept softly like sound through the
    gloom—
  'Twas the first fall of snow.

The Poet looked forth from his eminent cell,
And the pavement shew'd white as the couch of a king;
Ah, once had that hour—he remembers it well,
  Been as welcome as spring !
To-morrow had seen him on cliff and in glen,
Bright missiles of silver victoriously throw ;
To-morrow had seen him rear castles and men
  From that first fall of snow !

Does boyhood yet bound where his steps are forgot?
Does Winter still smile where he jocundly ranged ?
His playmates—lament they that all in *their* lot
  Save the snow, has been changed ?
The hue of *their* hair, is it blighted to grey ?
The warmth of *their* limbs, is it ceasing to glow ?
In poverty's garb shrink *they* now in dismay
  At the first fall of snow !

O shame upon Fortune ! O out upon Life !
O hatred and scorn on the clouds and the sun !
No voice to lament where the shadows are rife
  But the musical one !
The balmiest of breath in the wilderness shed ;
The stream that springs purest first ceasing to flow ;
Each poison-tree green, and the roses all dead
  'Neath the first fall of snow !

O fearful, I ween, grows that pale watcher's frown,
  As his thought gathers shape in the desolate air ;
It points to the snow-flakes—it motions him down,
  And its name is—Despair.

*   *   *

'Tis morning—a lattice hangs open, and hark—
What questions unanswered are ringing below,
Where the drift sinks discolored, and something lies
    stark
  'Neath that first fall of snow!

JACK TRUELOVE.

Sailors, they say, are rovers gay,
  With hearts still shifting like the sea ;
But one I knew, of jacket blue,
  Who loved full well and constantly.
Home-scenes behind, his gentle mind
  On tropic wave or icy shore,
Would still recal, and 'mong us all
  Jack Truelove was the name he bore.

No mate he found, the world around,
  Like one within the English foam ;
No foreign fair, bore to compare,
  With her whom he had kissed at home.
And for that twain, from land and main,
  Of gifts he fain had formed a freight,
The Indian's skill tasking for Will,
  And rifling woods and caves for Kate.

And homeward now as turns our prow,
  He tells as how to crown his life,
That friend's to stand at his left hand,
  That darling Kate to be his wife.

Bright broke the day as oped the bay,
  The church-tower grey o'erlooked the strand,
Flashed to the shore the bending oar,
  Jack waved his hat and leaped to land.

But friendship here no haven clear
  Of secret shoals may hope to find,
And when the gale strikes Fancy's sail,
  Faith's anchor drags in Woman's mind;
His native glen treading again,
  How throbbed Jack's heart with transport rife,
How changed his cheer when he doth hear,
  That Will and Kate are man and wife!

Tars that are flung land sharks among,
  Soon find ashore but little ease,
So hastening back I shipped with Jack,
  To fight the Frenchman on the seas.
How had he sped? and was he wed?
  My messmate's lips gave brief reply.
While turned aside he sought to hide
  The silent answer of his eye.

And weeks had passed ere by the mast,
  Grasping my hand and groaning sore,
He did repeat his love's deceit,
  Then pledged me ne'er to name her more,
And from that night, fare as he might,
  His sorrow lay as dumb as death,
While other tongues took up his songs,
  And told old yarns of love and faith.

Nor aught his ear listed to hear,
  Save sounds betokening danger's tread,
The tempest hoarse thwarting our course,
  Or battle bellowing fierce a-head.

Then the light tone he had foregone,
  Was with the bursting storm restored;
Or once more gay he led the way,
  Soon as the word was passed—to board.

But though no foe with open blow,
  Might brave him on the bloody deck,
The faithless friend would often bend
  In midnight watch, his bronzed neck.
And still the most nigh cliff or coast,
  Seemed his old wrong from woman's lip,
In thought restored—ever aboard
  He stayed—Jack never left the ship.

There like the rest he did his best,
  Till England's proud unanswered gun
Proclaimed afar, at Trafalgar,
  Great Nelson's last of duties done.
Then home we go, a prize in tow,
  As pledge of that dread victory gained;
But where the waves roofed quiet graves,
  I trow Jack rather had remained.

Fair blows the wind; the Captain's kind;
  "Hark ye my lad," he says to Jack,
"Sweethearts and wives; the morn arrives,
  "They'll kiss and give us welcome back.
"Soon shall bright eyes salute our prize,
  "So leap aloft an ye be fain
"England to see upon the lee;"
  But Jack ne'er saw her cliffs again.

Up the tall mast he slowly passed,
  No lubber landsman climbs more slow,
Waved from his hand his native land,
  And sprang into the depths below.

Ye maidens pale who hear my tale,
Let it avail to keep you kind,
And still be loth to break your troth,
Bearing Jack Truelove in your mind.

LINES

SUGGESTED BY THE DISCOVERY OF THE PLANET NEPTUNE.

Lo! where the secret depths of heaven unfold
The star man's *mental* vision sooner saw,
To vindicate the prescience that foretold,
And reconcile anomaly with law.

Thus ne'er, within the shadows of our sphere,
O, faith, the soul's astronomer, despond,
But, e'en from doubts and perturbations here,
Wisely anticipate the *world beyond !*

LINES

ON THE VISIT OF IBRAHIM PACHA TO BELFAST.

From where old Nile expends his annual stores,
Between the pyramids that press his shores,
(At his soft touch recurrent plenty springs,
And shames the vain petrific pomp of kings);
From that rich region of indulgent earth,
Whose harvests boast an immemorial birth;
From that clear clime, where man's adoring eyes
First track'd the bright progressions of the skies;

From realms antique, where hist'ry founds her tale—
To these new walls—to this chill Western vale,
What tempts the heir of Pharaoh's throne to sail ?
This Prince—the leader of a pilgrim band—
This fiery warrior, with unweapon'd hand ?

Listen, ye proud ! nor thoughtlessly contemn—
He seeks our fields, to pull a textile stem ;
From the brown husk explore its lithe advance,
To the blue flower that bends beneath his glance ;
Discern the soil, the stream, delights it most,
And count each waving fibre at its cost.
Then, what, mature, has doff'd the shatter'd rind,
He hastes to view, where prompt to clasp and wind,
Machines work subtly, as replete with mind ;
Spin—snap the threads—commingle or oppose,
And limn the glist'ning canvas, as it grows.
Last, on the mead, lo ! *linen* lies complete,
Like sudden snows, around the stranger's feet.

What ! for such paltry sights, devoid of state,
Hath hither come our bearded Potentate ?
An Eastern Chief, with pipe and dirk array'd,
To note the march of husbandry and trade !
A three-tail'd Pacha, full of pride and wrath,
Peering, like pedlar, o'er a table-cloth !
His native industry all thrown a-back,
Its gems—its gold—the bowstring and the sack !
Allah ! should Moslem fancies stoop this way,
What will bazaars and harems think and say ?
Once, only once, he turn'd to lance and gun,
And carelessly, and when his *work* was done—
Heaven send his throne may prove a stable one !

Proceed, sage Prince, pluck wisdom as you roam,
Seize foreign arts, and lead the captives home.

Teach your great Sire the lessons learn'd afar,
And hide in *sheaves* his shining scimitar.
With olive fence protect his ample store,
Nor tempt the lightnings with your laurels more.
Tell him his old antagonists abhor
With rival zeal th' " untoward" game of war,
And with kind emulation, now compete
In finding means to make *existence* sweet—
To speed the plough, secure the lab'ring keel,
Propel the car along its path of steel,
Relieve the weak, reward the working hand,
And trust in *Freedom* to *protect* the Land,
For ends like these e'en British Statesmen bend,
Nor shrink from change, when Reason cries "amend."

And if when England, France, have found their fame,
Poor Ireland! Mehemet should drop *thy* name,
Let him be told our records point of yore,
A Chief—Milesius, anchoring on his shore,
To win its fruits, and meditate its lore.
That fondly retrospective, Erin yet
Remembers this hereditary debt,
And of the science long to Egypt due,
Restored some portion, Ibrahim, to *you*,
You who adopt each art with fost'ring care,
Nor struck at *Commerce*, when your sword was bare.

Spirit of peace! beneficently bland,
Confirming States—cementing land to land,
And teaching love with knowledge to expand ;
Spirit of industry ! whose fictile force
Wins for creation's self a wider course,
And 'portioning sage, the sun—the soil—the rain—
Mellows each fruit, and multiplies each grain ;

Improves the ore—the fibre nature lent,
And craves but *room* to better her intent;
Then speeds the varied *goods* from pole to pole,
To cheer, sustain, and elevate the whole.
Oh, ye bless'd sisters! War's fell banners furl'd,
Spread your benign dominion o'er the world!
Round Ibrahim's steps with grateful omens smile,
From dusky Egypt to the Emerald Isle,
And bind one aidful neighbourhood of men
From Cairo's sun-scorched towers to Collin's leafy glen!

THE FAIR IRISH FACE.

(A Ballad.)

I.

The moon show'd her shield as the chief closed his
    round,
Where the standard fell low o'er the ramparted
    ground,
And arms glitter'd watchful from bastion and height,
To be traced on the dawn by a deadlier light.
'Twas the eve of the May, and the wreath that she
    wrought,
Is twining again in that veteran's thought,
As o'er long years of exile it flies for a space
To the home of his youth—to a fair maiden's face.

II.

" Whose voice, like our leader's, still prompted to dare,
When Hope, grown forlorn, left her task to Despair?
Whose tongue, like O'Donnell's, is tuned to record
The legends of valour that sharpen the sword?"—

The chieftain heard coldly his comrades' request,
For the echoes of battle lay hush'd in his breast,
And his tale—'twas the last he was doom'd to retrace—
Had no sterner theme than a fair maiden's face.

III.

"Fifty summers have fled"—it was thus he began,
With a soft tone and glance for a war-nurtur'd man—
"Since that sunny May morn, still so vividly seen,
When, a stalwart young peasant, I danced on the green
With her"—and his sabre uplifted flashed far—
"Whose mem'ry shines yet like yon motionless star;
Her features, her name, time but deepens their trace—
'Twas a soft Irish name—'twas a fair Irish face.

IV.

"How fleet sped my wooing! how oft in my tent
Has the night-wind repeated her whispered assent!
Short and low as that pledge was, and timidly given,
Yet it held upon earth, and 'twill bind us in Heaven.
We loved as none love, but in peril and need;
For, baited by bloodhounds of Sasanach breed,
Our country lay groaning .and grief and disgrace
Changed the hue of the rose on each fair Irish face.

V.

"What a fate have the Irish abroad or at home!
'Tis as slaves to remain—'tis as *strangers* to roam—
No shore hath the sun seen so fair, so unblest,
When he pours his *last* beams on the Isle of the West.
Loved daughter of Erin! lost pulse of my heart!
We heard at the altar the signal to *part*—
And the ban of the foe broke the outlaw's embrace
When he kiss'd a bride's tears from the fair Irish face.

VI.

"The traitors were baffled—the ocean was cross'd—
My life it was saved, but its happiness lost;
Though for fealty and force, as this sword could record,
In all lands, except one, there are trust and reward:
But *there* drooped the eyes I had taught so to mourn,
Thence a desolate voice seemed still sobbing 'return!'
O! wild sprung my heart as my charger in chase,
When it throbb'd once again towards the fair Irish face."

VII.

He paus'd—then resum'd, as if mem'ry had wept—
"The trysting was sad, and 'twas dismally kept;
We met—yes, we met, when long years had ta'en wing,
But not 'neath the hawthorn, but not in the spring—
The pale light that fell through the comfortless air,
On a low grave gleam'd fitfully—Oonagh was *there*:
And the sere grass of Autumn waved high o'er the place,
Where the soft Irish turf hid the fair Irish face.

VIII.

"No rust dims my sword, but I'm weary of strife—
My thoughts lose their way 'neath the shadows of life;
Hope's banner that guided them ceases to wave,
And glory shews dim from the edge of the grave.
Yet still, as of old, my heart's pulses are stirr'd,
By the mem'ry, though mute, of a musical word—
A vision long fled, I still pine to retrace—
'Tis a soft Irish name, 'twas a fair Irish face."

KOSSUTH.

1851.

He came, that pale Chief, from his prison afar,
　With no bribe to inveigle, no splendour to charm;
He came with defeat on his brow, like a scar,
　And the stigma of manacles fresh on his arm.

On an isle that sits calm in the turbulent sea,
　That waif of misfortune a moment was thrown;
And the welcome that spoke *it* the land of the free
　Now rings throughout Europe to lib'rate his own.

How close was he clasp'd to the Briton's broad breast!
　How the English hurrah spread his fame to the air!
How vied the swart cities in zeal to attest
　That the stranger—oh, no!—that the *patriot* was there!

How that foreigner's narrative kindled applause,
　When the tale of his "poor country's" contest was
　　caught!
How silence condoled with that fugitive's pause,
　When grief broke an eloquence Shakspeare had
　　taught!

For no weak regret from those firm lips was heard;
　Nor banquet exordiums forgot as they fall:
'Twas an orator spoke, but each vehement word
　Had the life of a hero as pledge for it all.

The demagogue's touch fell benumbed from a hand
　That had battled for order, and wrestled for laws;
While diadems saved not from "perjury's" brand,
　Affixed by the "true to humanity's cause."

"Peace follows contentment" (weigh, Kings, the re-
    mark !);
" And in Liberty's garden alone grows content ;"
Thus Truth through his lips flashed her maxims, and hark
    How the thunder rolls round of the nations' assent !

Unto Kaisar and Czar 'mid their fastnesses grim,
    That ready response flies a sentence of guilt ;
But 'tis melody *here*, and 'twill swell like a hymn
    In yon strong fane of freedom, by Washington built.

Plead on, O Kossuth ! While thy accents of flame
    Are welding the souls of the Saxon and Hun,
Lo, the strength of earth's tyrants is turning to shame !
    Lo, the glaciers shrink back at the touch of the sun !

ABD-EL-KADER AND LOUIS PHILIPPE.

A RHAPSODY.

1848.

" Our African captive, now vainly enraged,
Shall soon bless the compact that caught him, and caged,
Nor growl o'er a promise but meant to ensnare,
When Paris has taught him *her* façon de faire."

So spake each pert Frenchman, with simper and leer ;
So spake each false Frenchman, with insolent sneer ;
So spake the *crowned* Frenchman, the meanest on earth,
Whilst shook his foul throne with his cynical mirth.

The Son of the Desert, the Nurseling of War—
He cringe in a palace—*he* court a boudoir !
Forego Freedom's thirst for the froth of your bowls,
Or the babble that empties your frivolous souls !

Wile forward and back at your fickle demand
The wave([5]) that breaks constant on Africa's strand;
Seduce o'er her wastes your pale lilies to bloom,
And scent with their languishing breath, the Simoom.

Train lions, like poodles, to fawn and to wince;
Teach pity to Frenchmen, or faith to their Prince;
But seek not an Arab your pupil to be,
And barter for bonbons the *right* to be free.

O, knew ye what pastime his wishes recal,
Ye would shrink from his side at the banquet and ball;
O, wot ye what revels in slumber he keeps,
Ye would fetter his sinewy arm as he sleeps.

The desert—the desert—it glads him in dreams,
There yet, unsurrendered, the scimitar gleams;
And 'scaped the false hand that was laid on his mane,
The war courser stretches the shadowy rein.

The combat—the combat—French rancour and guile
Are writhing their last in that visioned defile;
There Isly remarshals her massacred men;
There Dahra's dread ashes are warring again!

He leads the grim band, and his falchion is red,
And the foe it last cleft had a crown on his head,
And that host, like a vapour, rolls backward, and breaks,
Shout, Freedom is won!—He awakes—he awakes.

Ah, woeful awaking! such ever was due
For all who were lulled, sordid Bourbon, by you;
Who trusted, as safeguards, 'gainst Liberty's loss,
Your promise, a bubble; your honour, a cross.

E'en Paris, cajoled by the vows that you spent,
Has found that *immuring* was all that they meant;
That the charter you ratified did but avail
For confirming the governorship of a gaol.

And hark! even now, her mistake to repair,
The tocsin—the tocsin, returns on the air;
Her fortress-girt precinct no stranger invades,
Yet again, in her blood-bedrenched streets, barricades!

And the tyrant turns pale, and his minions are prone,
And rebellion has laid a red hand on the throne.
Fling it forth to the flames! 'tis not meet to behold
How he sullied its purple, and pilfered its gold.

O, Nemesis! he of contrivance discreet,
To occupy, ere it was vacant, that seat;
Who prompted its foes till his kinsman withdrew,
Then mounted—*he* now is a fugitive too.

He, chosen by Freedom her treasures to save,
Has broken *against* her the sceptre she gave;
He, pledged to the nations their rights to regain,
Hears now but accusers from Poland to Spain.

Let him live—'tis a sentence than death more severe,
For his profitless falsehoods to hiss in his ear;
And an exile's regrets his vain cunning upbraid
With each friend it debased, with each foe it betrayed.

Let him live with no hope to alleviate his doom,
That oblivion shall shadow his reprobate tomb,
Or infamy cease the reproach to renew
Of you, Isabel, Abd-el-Kader, of you.

THE RIGHT OF WAY.

Of all her creatures here below
  Nature consorts the place and plight;
Assimilates the hue to snow;
  Associates the eye with light;
Grants to each lower want a zone
  Whence instinct sure forbids to stray;
But gives to reasoning man alone
  O'er the whole earth a "right of way."

No bounds prescribed to bird or brute
  May 'gainst their sovereign's stride prevail;
What mountain but hath kissed his foot?
  What sea saluteth not his sail?
Whilst tamed, the car or keel to urge,
  The elements his beck obey,
Jungle, morass, ice, sand, or surge—
  Which may contest his "right of way?"

Nor to a free material course
  Is the great wanderer's claim confined;
Endowed with like pervasive force
  Proceeds th' investigating mind.
Where justice high her scales suspends,
  Where knowledge sheds her genial ray,
Where freedom's sword her cause defends,
  God gives to man the "right of way."

But ah! despite such charter wide,
  The earth is rough with barriers still,
Greed still *protects* the Port, and pride
  Defends, from *naked* foot, the hill.
Tyrants, whom servile fears control,
  Still cage brave hearts that spurn their sway;
Still bigot priests would chain the soul,
  And bar to Heaven its "right of way."

Whilst Faith and Love, blest twins, accord
　Each page and path uniting men,
That Tuscan prince—this Scottish lord—
　Proscribes the Bible—shuts the glen!
And mark, by yon embattled strand,
　The famished camp—the freighted bay—
O! England, there thy trammell'd hand
　To France resigned its "right of way!"

Advance, reform! on every track
　Let in opinion's sifting air!
The politician's *cul-de-sac*
　Change to the patriot's thoroughfare!
Religion, spread thy beams divine!
　The tinted lattice streaks the day;
Too much the screen before the shrine
　Obstructs the votary's "right of way."

————

SONNETS TO A GIG.

Not the precipitate wings of Icarus,
　Nor Jove's own eagle clutching at my cloak,
　Nor menaceful Medea's *drag-on* yoke
(Set up when bilked of her spouse's *bus*);
Not the confounded Phaëtonic fuss,
　Nor Bacchus' *tiger'd* curricle that broke
　Down, when Frère Mathew a pernicious spoke
Clapp'd in its wheel.   By none of these, nor thus
Would *I* be borne; nor would it sweetly strike
　My fancy to be drawn through air or sea
　By dove or dolphin; also unto me
Europa's courser seems unladylike.
In thee, O Gig, first sat there, straight as pike,
Unmythical respectability!

There are, O Gig, who vilify thy mien
As 'wulgar'—haply that in draggled plight,
Where sign-board low waves welcome to the night,
At tail of foundered steed thou hast been seen;
Or that by Sunday Jehu (Boult or Green);
Or butcher truculent from fair or fight;
Or flippant bagman with cigar alight;
Or gauger testifying of poteen,
Close to their toes was splashed thy sudden wheel,
Startling them smirched to execrate his eyes.
What then? shall we completely stigmatize
Buds for their cankers? for its maggots, meal?
Distain not mists the chariot of the skies?
Conveys not Earth much—much of ungenteel?

THE REFORMATORY.

"God said, 'Let there be light,' and ——."—*Book of Genesis.*
"Under the lamp it is dark."—*Arabian Proverb.*

Knowledge spreads—from height to height
Leaps th' illimitable light;
O'er the sombre moor advances;
'Thwart the sordid alley glances;
Where it brightens, hate and dolour,
Rising, lose their livid colour;
Labour's brow serener flushes;
Error owns the beam in blushes;
Tears fall softly, whilst above
Radiates clear the arch of love.

Knowledge spreads—yet still we find
Wanderers many dazed or blind :
Thralls of ignorance whose plight
Shows but darker for the light ;
Baleful barrenness more drear
For the jocund harvests near ;
There the lustrous fields sustain
Blossoms sweet and foodful grain ;
Huddle *here* in daylight scant
Fungus foul and poison-plant !

How shall we such wildings tame ?
How this moral waste reclaim ?
Or, to slight the withering weed,
How confine its noxious seed ?

Pass th' unseemly outcasts by
With prudish or prudential eye,
Satisfied some nooks to spare
For vice to shoot his rubbish there ?
Prosecute the easy plan
Aloof to pity or to ban?
Or, to abate and render pure,
Approach the nuisance, and immure ?
Harrow the tainted soil, or draw
Round it the sharpened spikes of law ?

No—to eradicate such ill
Unkindly means were futile still :
Early hath been tried, and late,
All the husbandry of *Hate*—
Still the vices germinate :
Procreant still 'gainst fence or frown,
Sin flings wide its thistle-down ;
Transplant, tear off—the stem, the leaf
But spreads the blight of guilt and grief ;

Sever or crush the noisome shoot,—
The pest rebourgeons from the root!

Truce to these emblems,—they suggest
Perdition for the peccant breast!
The tares that nobler growths annoy
'Tis *Agriculture* to *destroy;*
Culture *humane* that would *restore,*
Drops there the cruel metaphor!

Love, his prime mission to improve,
Is, e'en in reprobating, Love;
But much prefers to bless than blame—
To rear to virtue, than reclaim;
To feed, with nurture timely lent,
The pure, than starve the penitent.
For, as the breast, the babe we find,
And knowledge is the milk of mind;
Contract or vitiate its supplies,
The nursling is deformed or dies;
Free be the stream, and fondly given,
How blooms the spirit-child of Heaven!

Alas for those would vainly sip!
Alas for many an arid lip!
Woe, woe confirmed, if life endure,
For Ignorance and Guilt *mature!*
Mature with soul-thirst unappeased,
Stunted, distorted, and diseased.
In cellarage of odium pent,
With orts obscene for nutriment,
And effluence foul of moral mud
To poison the impoverished blood.
Truth, by *their* reason, viewed awry,
Their conscience—to *conceal* the lie,

Of justice to elude the rod,
Nor own, save in blaspheming, God!
Such Pariahs who but will contemn?
Who owns fraternity with them?
What art to health or hope may train
Such Cretins of the heart and brain?

As pious Islamite will spare
To burn the casual page, or tear,
Lest "Allah" should be written there,
So, on each human waif of shame,
Let faith surmise its maker's name,
Assume the heart of marred design,
May yet hold something of divine;
And, in its desecrated plan
The criminal but *blur* the man.
Then haply from its miry bed
Shall Pity raise the vagrant shred;
Discover, in the soul debased,
Contrition's rubric faintly traced;
Find, to renew with reverent care,
Religion's faded impress there;
Yea, hold redeemed from stain and strife,
A fragment of the Book of Life!

SONNETS.

ON THE PICTURE OF A BOY SHOOTING AT A TARGET.

'Twas deftly aimed, young archer! fairly sped.
Thine arrow blots the target's inmost ring;
Thy heart the while, with emulative spring,
Blaz'ning the triumph which thy bow hath bred:

Not Phœbus loftier brow'd, the Python dead;
  Not brighter eyed the Love god on the wing,
  When having smitten the Olympian king,
To Venus' smile he turns his wanton head.
Yet ah, whilst on this pictur'd semblance sweet
  I gaze, what sterner vision thwarts my glance?
    What archers these, so menaceful and dark?
Lo, from where gath'ring clouds presageful meet,
  Grim-quiver'd forms relentlessly advance,
    Sorrow, and pain, and death—and thou, sweet boy,
    the *mark*.

How many shafts are shot the world around!
  How many hearts the archers' skill attest!
  A victim bleeds in every human breast;
No nook but where some quarry sinks astound.
This earth, me thinks, is fortune's hunting ground,
  And fearful men her miserable quest,
  Whom, led by her, and to her will address'd,
Fleet griefs and fanged passions snare and wound.
Love, the lithe pestilence that early clings;
  Revenge, the blood hound staunch of ranc'rous jaws;
Wild jealousy, far borne on gryphon wings;
  Oppression's tiger train, despising laws;
  The woe that crushes, and the want that gnaws;
Pain's writhing brood, and guilt's severer stings!

NOT GONE YET.

"Wave, ye dark tresses! clust'ring, or apart,
  Contrast your beauty with the snowy brow;
Ringlets no more are fetters for my heart,
  Nor doth it tremble with their motion now.

Smile, ye bright eyes! your wanton beams no more
  Shall wrongfully divert a glance of mine;
My bark is turn'd from Love's illusive shore,
  And its false lights now unregarded shine."
But whilst the mariner in boastful joy,
  Again afloat, his sails is shaking out,
Lo! at the helm there stands a Winged Boy,
  And silently the ship is put about.

FEUDALITY.

The Feudal System—pride and shame
Must still contest that dubious name,
Plumed valour boast his efforts crown'd,
And freedom shudder at the sound.
The Feudal System—force and wrong
In tower and donjon built it strong,
And clank of chains, and clash of swords,
Reverb'rate in those iron words.

From fortress grim that fenced above
The narrow limits of his love,
Of wide domains the only part
Which own'd allegiance of the *heart;*
Enforcing far each stern demand
By title of a sheathless brand;
Gold, freedom, life, in his award,
How proudly sway'd the feudal *lord!*

But 'neath such despot man became
The vile in nature, as in name;
Spurned back from battle's bright array,
To burrow in his kindred clay;
Or flung in scorn from lance to lance,
A churlish soil's appurtenance;

His life a stain, his soul a grave,
How wretched crouched the feudal *slave!*

It pass'd—Religion's sacred breath
Slowly dissolved that rule of death;
Some gleams of letter'd wisdom caught,
Subdued fierce minds to milder thought;
The spreading links which traffic bound,
Knit patriots, too, on common ground,
Till fear reposed as gen'rous awe,
And force was rectified to law.

The Feudal Times—those times are flown,
Power leans not now on steel or stone,
Escaping from his lonely den,
The serf 's become the citizen.
Society, one pervious whole
For all the lightnings of the soul,
Bursts the coarse bondage it abhorr'd,
And crowns *opinion* as its lord.

"AND THE FAMINE WAS SORE IN THE LAND."

1847.

Where hoarse th' Atlantic billow raves
 On southmost Cork's dejected strand,
What cry outsounds the troubled waves?
 The wailing of a famish'd land.
Whilst borne from every bleak abode,
 As Winter rears his icy wall,
The same funeral accents load
 The mountain blasts of Donegal.

The songs that made our hearths rejoice,
  Pale Woman's lip no longer pours;
Whilst manhood's hesitating voice
  For bread—bread only—now implores.
For bread life's sinking powers to nurse—
  Bread which the *hand* would earn in vain,
Till earth with mitigated curse
  Bid baffled Labour *strive* again.

On his lone threshold see him stand,
  That pining peasant spectre-thin;
Without, his rood of traitor land;
  Starvation and despair within.
His wife—his babes—his festered food,
  Her urgent plaint—*their* failing breath—
Ah, shield that wretch from thoughts of blood!
  That hut reprieve from sin and death!

Much, much the meanest boon avails
  When "famine clings" in dubious strife;
A crust of bread may fix the scales,
  Where tremble innocence and life.
One ray of sympathy supplied,
  Correct a brain that darksome erred;
Revive a heart that, longer tried,
  Had frozen been from warmth deferred.

By gentle stress—with patient skill,
  Each link of human wrong is loosed;
The mountain mass of human ill
  By pity's slend'rest stream reduced.
And, lightened thus, misfortune shows
  The purpose of her earthly yoke,
Pointing a meaning for our woes
  In every virtue they evoke.

If, Erin, thine abortive toil
  Have yielded yet a warning wise;
If from the ruins of thy soil
  A *moral* harvest shall arise;
If prudence, vigour, justice lost,
  Thence renovate thy growth of *men*,
Though dear the rigid culture cost
  The fruit will recompence thee then.

TO EMMA.

WITH A COPY OF MRS. JAMESON'S " COMMON-PLACE
BOOK OF THOUGHTS, MEMORIES, AND FANCIES."

" Thoughts, Memories, Fancies" exquisitely traced,
Loose blooms of Genius caught and fixed by Taste:
With Feeling's tendrils fastened ere they fall,
Here meet, and blend into a coronal
Artistically twined, yet sweetness all:
Shedding mild sapience whilst so fair to see,
And thus an offering, Emma, meet for Thee.
Fancies and thoughts the brightest, most benign,
Irradiate her who prompts the best of mine:
The choicest memories recompense in part,
The Wife who stores such in her husband's heart;
Love must be hers;—without whose eyes to read,
Our leaves of life were ' common-place' indeed!

SONG.

I sit in a palace on Italy's strand,
  The wine in my chalice, the lute in my hand;
But the strain that I sing is from far o'er the sea,
"Aileen mavourneen, a cuishla machree!"

For high halls revealing their splendour in vain,
My lone mountain shieling now holds me again,
And gems, gold, and marble, O foreign are ye
To " Aileen mavourneen, a cuishla machree !"

Though flattery woo me, it wins no reply ;
Though love may bend to me, I yield but a sigh ;
'Tis a sigh for the whisper, beneath the old tree,
" Aileen mavourneen, a cuishla machree."

Loved land of my childhood ! its waywardness o'er,
This heart once so wild, would now break on thy shore
If to soothe its last throbbings once more I might be
" Aileen mavourneen, a cuishla machree."

MEDICAL RECIPE.

By a patient too fair sate a doctor too young,
With eyes more intent on her lips, than her tongue ;
He tested her heart, as its pulse's recorder,
But, alas ! in his own was the latent disorder ;
And soon from the region in which it was bred,
That sad " tremor cordis " so muddled his head,
That instead of some physic to mend her condition,
He urg'd as a recipe, take your Physician !

DIRGE.

Thou art dying ! In those eyes,
  Fixed so wistfully above,
Beams a reflex of the skies,
  Whither thou art hast'ning, love.
And that dim unbraided hair,
And that brow too purely fair,

ι

And that cheek of wasteful glow,
　And those lips of lavish breath;
Thus doth mortal beauty show
　In the dawn of death!

Few the years, and fewer seeming,
　Since a mother's arms were press'd
Round the balmy heaven-dreaming
　Of thine infant rest!
Now thy latest couch is strown,
Now shalt thou in lying down,
Realise those visions flown.

Gather cowslips from the mead,
　Steal the violet from her cell,
Weave a garland for the dead,
　Of rose and asphodel,
Orange bloom, and myrtle wave
For the bridal of the grave,
Lasting amaranth let it have!

Time abjures his task of blighting,
　Dim-ey'd Time the stern and hoary;
Death his rich right hand is plighting,
　Death, who opes the gate of glory;
Gleams from thence around him grouping
O'er his young betrothed, drooping,
Lo! the mighty angel stooping!

Now within his arms she's lying
　Gazing on a farther sun,
Now for ever's hush'd the sighing
　Of our pale and pensive one.
Never more shall grief or fear
Stain her with an earthly tear;
Come away, she is not here!

THE EARTH-MAIDEN.

Down, down, a thousand fathoms down,
  In sea-cave deep, that plummet scorneth;
Oh! that I wore a coral crown,
  Such as the Nereid's brow adorneth!
High, high, above the mountain's height,
  Beneath whose crest the chill mist halteth,
Would that I waved a wing of light,
  Such as the Nymph of air exalteth!

Calm in an ebbless tide of peace,
  Floats the soft minion of the water;
Serene, where jarring tempests cease,
  Soars the light Sylph, the sunbeam's daughter.
But the Earth-maiden, the unwise,
  Ah! me, her throbbing breast is telling
Nought of the bright air, but the sighs,
  Nought of the cool wave, save the swelling.

PARTING.

Oh! the ill-dissembled pangs of parting!
The eyes averted, while the tears are starting,
The smile compulsive, and the sigh compressed,
The *busying*, to hide the tortur'd breast;
The feeble effort to confirm and cheer,
When all is mutual sorrow, mutual fear.
The happiness recalled with sunken brow,
And broken voice, for it is over now!
The sobbed assurance of such yet to come,
Whilst in this hour of severance, hope is dumb;
Oh! the ill-dissembled pangs of parting,
The lips faint smiling, while the tears are starting!

Oh! the tokens all too plain of parting
The restless step,—the tremulous exerting,
The seeking for pretexts to linger on,
The over-pained impatience to be gone,
The long-fixed gaze on the beloved face,
The desperation of the last embrace!
Hands that would still be joined, despite of fate,
Lips that would cling too close to separate,
Hearts of one beat, 'tis past; at length ye sever,
Pale, cold, despairing, brokenly, for ever!
Oh! the bitter, bitter pangs of parting,
The shadows of a world the sun's deserting!

AN EXCELLENT NEW BALLAD, CALLED

"A LESSON TO PADDY;"

*Respectfully dedicated to the Commissioners of National Education, by
Dionysius O'Toole, Philomath, Barony of Ballymawhack, Co. Sligo.*

The national evils that sprout in
  This island, I've studied, each shoot of them,
And am satisfied past any doubtin,
  That prosody lies at the root of them,
I heed not the dunce's ha, ha;
  For the first letter proves what I say,
Don't the Irish forever roar, ah!
  While the English squeak constantly, eh!
    Now is that any way to converse?

Walking up through grammatical nature,
  And to nouns our next notice assigning,
Substantial ones, Paddy the crature
  Has a wonderful knack of declining;

Th' accusative's his in all places,
  The ablative's mighty oppressive;
But of all the impossible cases,
  He never can learn the possessive,
        And so he is foot of his class.

If verbs, I be airing him through them,
  His road it grows rougher and rougher,
For to Be, and have nothing to Do then,,
  Says he, can mean only to suffer.
His moods are so changeable still,
  He can't keep them fixed for an hour,
And confounding the Shall and the Will,
  He next takes the will for the pow'r,
        And holds out his hand for his pains.

If the tenses he's set on declaiming,
  Of the Past he hooks up some old story,
For the Present, he's absently dreaming
  Of some paulo-post Future of glory;
As for Voices, his still is for fun,
  Though certain to suffer condignly;
And if blamed for his Carryings-on,
  He just floors the master Supinely,
        Such a genius for grammar has Pat.

Yet he'll somehow insense you, it's equal
  If wishing to serve, or to fight one,
" Clear the road!" or " You're welcome!" the sequel
  You'll find is the logical right one.
To conjugate early he shows too
  Infinitive aptness of functions,
He's pat in his Ahs, and his Ohs, too,
  And he is the dab at conjunctions.
        There he still does be prompting the girls.

Arrah! Pat, if you'd heed my advising,
   I'd make you the pride of Parnassus,
Don't you see how the Head does keep rising,
   While the hands and the feet toil like asses?
Put that stick you are flourishing, down,
   Or fight for some reason assignable,
You mighty irregular noun,
   With that adjective so indeclinable!
      It's a construin' you want, with the taws.

Oh! the curse of the crows on bad teaching!
   Man and boy, it has been your disaster;
By that vagabond Bull's over-reaching,
   You could not have had a worse Master.
To make you agree he begins
   Like some Ingin, to teach you the war-dance,
If your Syntax tax'd none of his sins,
   His government broke your concordance,
      And then he flogg'd on at his ease.

He turn'd you to dine in the ditches,
   And lash'd you for daring to mutter,
What, if you had no piatees or breeches,
   So his dirty bread got its butter.
Now, Pat, you're too big for the rogue,
   So cease both to snivel and stammer;
Speak up! never blush for your brogue,
   But hold on by your National Grammar,
      And you'll yet be the Cock of the School.
      Quod testor, D. O'T., *Schol. Rector.*

LOUIS NAPOLEON.

November, 1852.

Empire for him!   For that ignoble front,
The supreme blazon of th' imperial band!
Napoleon's sceptre in that sordid hand,
And France shouting the *name* as she was wont!
Is not this he who fill'd young Freedom's font
With innocent blood?   With perjuries like sand,
Choked her weak breath, and on yon pois'nous strand
Flung the true sponsors whom he failed to daunt?
  Is not this he who forged, and robbed, and slew,
Projecting each cold crime with politic zest?
O sword of Justice, fallest thou so wide!
  Such Ruler's infamy his country's too,
On this her basest son, as if the best,
France smiles, and *crowns* that foul Liberticide!

VERSES,

CHIEFLY TRANSLATIONS,

BY

WILLIAM DRENNAN.

VERSES,

CHIEFLY TRANSLATIONS,

BY

WILLIAM DRENNAN.

CATHAL CROIVDEARG* O'CONOR.

In the Church of Knock Moy see a Grey-friar stand,
One pale hand to his brow ; *that* was once a red hand,
For the sword it uplifted but fell to destroy,
As the Sassenach knew on thy summit, Knock Moy!
But the Friar now kneels, where the Warrior stood,
And the house of the Lord hides the hillock of blood ;
The red hand that erst scatter'd the foes of the Gael,
Thin and worn, props a penitent visage, and pale ;
The wars of Cathal Croivdearg O'Conor have ceas'd,
Save that of the spirit that prays for a priest,
And the priest prays for it, when an abbey is giv'n,
Requiescat in pace ; and after, in heaven !
For here is the record the shavelings have writ,
And it seems worth a moment's attention to it,
For it reads like a good many texts from such schools,
Too simple for knaves, and too worldly for fools.
"He led from the date of the death of his wife,
A singular, single, and virtuous life ;

* Red Hand.

He destroy'd far more traitors than any before,
And supported far more of the Clergy, and Poor.
He died full of good, as he lived free of evil
A conqueror over the World, and the Devil,
Whose rage against pious O'Conor was vain;
Note—that Tithes were first lawfully paid in
  his reign !"

OF ART MAC MORROGH, (O'CAVENAGH), AND HOW HE BAFFLED THE ENGLISH KING, RICHARD II.

'Twas at Kenlis in Kilkenny, where the Saxon forces
  fell,
With Roger Mortimer himself who led them on to hell;
His heirdom to the haughty crown of England nought
  avail'd,
But King Richard to avenge him with two hundred ships
  hath sail'd,
The standard of St. Edward waves o'er forty thousand
  men,
Marching on; will Art Mac Morrogh ever take the field
  again ?
Nay, not with bare three thousand, but within his house
  he stood,
The castle God had rear'd for him, the free and glad-
  some wood !
And methinks you might as well attempt to chain the
  mountain breeze,
As capture Kerne or Gallowglass, while the leaves are
  on the trees.

So king Richard now may fight his fill with forest, bog
and lake,
But never, flounder as he will, the Irish overtake;
Tho' they have oft, those savages, such fleetness and
such force,
As to catch an English steed, and drag the rider off
his horse!
So saith Froissart; no Gasconade, oh Saxon, I indite,
Tho' now I give the very words of a gallant Gascon
Knight.
" We strive the woods to burn and hew, the villages
to fire,
But our soldiers when they would pursue, sink to their
reins in mire,
While the enemy hang on us and harass us front and rear,
And rain and wind, with want and cold starve steed
and cavalier.
Yet while they had enough to eat, was nought our men
could vex,
So that many foes submitted, and with halters round
their necks ;
And the king to Art Mac Morrogh sent that he should
do the same,
But from that Irish Chief the high and haughty answer
came,
That for all the gold the world could hold an inch he
would not yield,
But make us feel with fire and steel his mast'ry in the
field,
But this audacious challenge was from knowing in his
wood,
That the very number of our Force had left us short of food,
Till one biscuit in a day was good allowance for five
men,
And I wish'd myself, the sooth to say, in Paris back
again,

Aye, back again in Paris, with no penny in my
purse,
Since Knights endur'd and Gentlemen, this miserable
curse.
Soon after, victual-laden, came from Dublin vessels
three,
And our famine-stricken soldiers rush'd upon them
thro' the sea;
The rugging and the ryving there was a beastly scene
I wot,
While many a curse and cuff they gave, and many more
they got,
Thereon the King dislodg'd, and march'd toward Dublin
on the morn,
While the Celts pursue with fearful howls, with skir
mish, scathe, and scorn;
But Mac Morrogh craves a parley, and great joy had we
I trow,
And I prick'd forth with many more to view our
mighty Foe.
Between two woods the sea hard bye, upon a bare-
back'd steed,
He gallop'd headlong down a hill, like hare or stag in
speed,
'Twas said the horse he rode had cost four hundred
Head of Kine,
But for all the cows in Christendom, had that good horse
been mine,
I had not ridden in cold blood, tho' no poltroon, thank
God!
As down that rugged mountain brow Mac Morrogh
madly rode;
A swarm of Irish follow'd close, until he near'd the
wood,
And a mighty dart right deftly cast, and then behind
him stood.

The Earl of Gloucester there he met, beside a little
 ford,
And many a dark-brow'd Norman eye on his mien and
 feature lower'd.
Both tall he look'd, and strongly knit, yet agile too as
 strong,
His face severe, and fierce his glance; the parley lasted
 long,
Much words for little matter; to his horde return'd
 Mac Morrogh,
And King Richard on to Dublin, boiling o'er with rage
 and sorrow.
Ere I leave Ireland's coast, he cried, he's mine alive or
 dead;
A hundred marks in gold, for Art Mac Morrogh, or his
 Head!
And if the woods were bare or burn'd, brave words
 forsooth were these,
But wind in my opinion—while the leaves were on the
 trees.
Howbeit, after scenes of such starvation and affright,
We all remain'd six weeks in dainty Dublin with delight,
But from England had no tidings, a very wond'rous
 thing,
And a presage as I deem'd that God was angry with
 the king;
The wind might be contrarious, and the weather foul
 and sore,
Yet why was this allow'd by heav'n—save as I said
 before?
For after long delay the wild winds at last went down,
And King Richard sail'd to lose his life, and ere his
 life, his Crown;
While Mac Morrogh, as in France I heard, liv'd many
 years at ease,
*And ever beat the English, when the leaves were on
 the Trees.*"

SONNET TO IRELAND.

Sad Inisfail! By Freedom never trode,
Save as some snowy sea fowl in its flight,
On storm-vex'd Barque a moment may alight,
And then forsake the thing giv'n o'er of God;
Victim of calm and tempest, force and fraud,
What common aim will e'er thy crew unite,
What hope or mem'ry steer their course aright,
Aliens at home, or parasites abroad?
Thine emblem, yon flush'd girl that flaunts along
Whose beauty lured the spoiler; for a space
She hears the prying stranger praise it still,
And glories in her shame; ev'n so the song
That lauds thee, Innisfallen, sounds disgrace,
While sooth'd or spurn'd at England's wayward will.

MEETING OF ESSEX AND TYRONE.

'Tis sunset; on this side, Earth's sorrows are past,
And her weary and worn ones may rest them at last,
And the head cease to ponder, the heart cease to grieve,
For night cometh with sleep; it is eve, it is eve!
And blithe feels the Sassenach soldier, out-worn
By a march that began with the waking of morn;
But 'tis over, halt, halt! is now echoed around,
For the leader hath chosen his bivouac ground.
The troopers dismount, and their chargers' shrill neigh,
Owns the pat, that says—"So much, old boy, for to-day!"
And the veteran foot soldier, standing at ease,
Mutters, " Aye, it may do," for before him he sees
The Brenna's steep bank, hanging rugged and high,
Like a dark brow that juts o'er a treacherous eye,

And the passes beyond scarce a bridle-path yield,
So knapsack and musket are piled on the field.
But hark! a faint regular tramp! it is gone,
It returns, low, then louder, then rattles right on,
To saddle! the Sassenach bugles have blown,
The Irish are on them, aboo with Tyrone!
Hurra! through the gorge like a whirlwind they wheel,
And the heart of the Saxon, tho' true as his steel,
Paus'd a beat, and then quicken'd its speed, as his foe
All reckless rush'd down the rude passes below,
Like a rock by the thunderbolt hurl'd from its throne,
And the first bounding fragment is Hugh of Tyrone.
Why starts the red soldier, and stands to his gun,
Doth Brenna less broad, or less rapidly run?
And why grips Earl Essex the hilt of his sword,
Is the spur of O'Nial a spell for a ford?
Yes, by Heav'n, see him plunge, while uncurb'd by the
        rein,
His black steed is breasting the current amain,
While those mad Irish Marcachs in motionless rank,
Look a living wall crowning the river's steep bank;
He crosses alone, and in wonder, I ween,
The minion, tho' brave, of the heretic Queen,
Gaz'd long, as reluctantly yielding belief,
On that wild Irish horse, and the wild Irish chief,
While more at his ease than Queen Bess on a throne,
Sate, soak'd in his saddle, the rebel Tyrone.
But his charger finds footing, and Hugh waves his
        hand,
Quoth the gallant young Earl, spurring on to the strand,
God's death! had his mother thrown doublets, old Bess
For a subject the more, had a kingdom the less!
And what was their parley? Let history tell!
Is she silent? I reck not; whate'er then befel,
The west-wind Earl Essex to England hath blown,
While scathless and free returned Hugh of Tyrone.

K

To regain the Queen's favor Earl Essex hath sped,
And succeeded at length—at the cost of his head;
Then too late she repents, and too late she forgives,
That spectre-thought haunts her last hours while she
    lives.
Her own peace hath perished; the peace of the State
Will come—for she never will learn it—too late.
Behold her, for days crouching down on the floor,
While her gray hair streams wildly, behind and before;
The desolate Lioness! Last of her race!
Remorse and fell hate sweep in turn o'er her face,
And despair gnaws her heart—is that squalid Distress,
That personified Misery—glorious Queen Bess?
Let enemies hasten to veil such a scene,
Lament for the woman, forgive e'en the Queen;
Hush! Elizabeth dies! a deep murmur—a groan, .
Her last sigh for Essex—her curse on Tyrone!

OWEN ROE O'NEILL AT BENBURB.

O'Neill is for his native land, and the faith she held of
    old;
Monroe is for the Parliament—the Scots, for Saxon
    gold;
Now have they heard as on they spurred, that Owen
    with his might,
Is at Benburb encamp'd—Benburb, of many a bloody
    fight;
Right early, ere the sun could rise, the morning march
    begun,
Of thousands who will close their eyes with yonder
    setting sun.

Lo, posted 'twixt two hills, O'Neill! a wood upon his
 rear,
The Blackwater upon his right, and in his front—who
 dare.
His cavalry upon the slope, like hawks upon his flanks
Hover'd before the deadly swoop that bore down hostile
 ranks;
Now the Scots have ta'en the water, at a ford close bye
 Kinard,
Their cry is—"Wha wi' us will mell, and what will us
 retard?"
Then Owen march'd a regiment to a pass upon their way,
But backward was the course it bent, when the cannon
 'gan to play;
For the plunging shot showr'd thick and hot, while
 comrades strew'd their track,
Yet in order good, as if review'd, fell the regiment
 slowly back.
Thought Owen Roe, the sun will glow towr'd ev'ning in
 our rear,
And in the faces of the foe with blinding eye-ball glare;
So, on at times he drew their pow'rs, and then he drove
 them back,
And thus he play'd with them for hours, nor gave them
 an attack,
Harassing them with skirmish, out-manœuvring poor
 Monroe;
Till at the sinking of the sun, uprose my Owen Roe!
The Scot on all sides baffled now, Retreat! had barely
 spoken,
When the Irish ranks dashed down the brow, and horse
 and foot were broken.
The sunburst in our banner, and the sunburst in our
 sky,
Sore choice was left the Scotchman sour; 'twas either
 fall, or fly;

Their coward-leader felt the last befitted best his kind,
And fleeing from the field so fast, left coat and wig
    behind.
But give our foes their due, his men fought dourly, ere
    they lay,
Heap'd scatter'd o'er the deadly hill, like laps of sum-
    mer hay.
Three thousand Scotch and English there are lying
    freshly slain,
And Blaney at his regiment's head will never charge
    again !
Montgomery is a captive, with gay officers a score,
While a hundred corpses only have the Irish to de-
    plore.
No longer Erin's sunburst shall a Scotchman's eye dis-
    turb,
Yet never pity him because he fell upon Benburb !
But think, that born 'neath his cold sky, upon his sterile
    land,
He yet found grace in fight to die, with the Irish hand
    to hand,
His bones in holy soil inurn'd ; say who would marvel
    not,
If homeward willingly return'd from Erin ere a Scot ?
The loon that ne'er a green tree view'd at home, were
    wise, I wis,
To end his life 'mid mead and wood, in such a land as
    this !
Then lasses cease to wail your lads ; your groans and
    greetings curb,
'Twas a lucky lot for the bonniest Scot to die upon
    Benburb.

THE BATTLE OF BEAL-AN-ATH BUIDH.

10th August, 1598.

I.

By O'Nial beleaguer'd, the spirits might droop
Of the Saxon three hundred, shut up in their coop,
Till Bagenal drew his Toledo, and swore,
On the sword of a soldier, to succour Portmore.

II.

His veteran troops, in the foreign wars tried—
Their features how bronzed, and how haughty their
    stride !—
Stept steadily on ; it was thrilling to see
That thunder-cloud brooding o'er BEAL-AN-ATH-BUIDH.*

III.

The flash of steel armour, inlaid with fine gold—
Gleaming matchlocks and cannon that muttering roll'd—
With the tramp and the clank of those stern cuirassiers,
Dyed in blood of the Flemish and French cavaliers.

IV.

Are the mere Irish, then, with pikes arrows, and
    darts—
With but glibb-cover'd† heads, and but rib-cover'd hearts,
Half-naked, half-fed, with few muskets, no guns—
The battle to dare against England's stout sons ?

* Town of the Yellow Ford.
† *Long hair twisted, so as to resist a sword cut.*

V.

Poor *Bonnochts*,* and wild Gallowglasses† and Kerns‡—
Let them war with rude brambles, sharp furze, and dry
    ferns !
Wirrastrue for their wives—for their babes *ochanie*,
If they wait for the Saxon at BEAL-AN-ATH-BUIDH !

VI.

Yet O'Nial stands firm—few and brief his commands—
Ye have hearts in your bosoms, and pikes in your hands:
Try how far ye can push them, my children, at once ;
Faugh-a-Ballagh !§—and down with horse, foot, and
    great guns.

VII.

They have gold and gay arms—they have biscuit and
    bread ;
Now, sons of my soul, we'll be found and be fed !
And he clutch'd his claymore, and "look yonder,"
    laughed he,
"What a grand commissariat for BEAL-AN-ATH-BUIDH !"

VIII.

Near the Chief, a grim tyke, an O'Shanaghan stood,
His nostril dilated seemed snuffing for blood ;
Rough and ready to spring, like the wiry wolf-hound
Of Ierné, who, tossing his pike with a bound,

IX.

Cried, "My hand to the Sassenach ! ne'er may I hurl
Another to earth, if I call him a churl !
He finds me in clothing, in booty, in bread—
My Chief, won't O'Shanaghan give him a *bed !*"

---

* *Military retainers.*   † Better sort of military.
‡ *Infantry poorly armed.*   § Fag-a-bealac—Clear the way.

x.

"Tir-Owen, abu!"* and the Irish rush'd on—
The foe gave but one volley—their gunners are gone.
Before the bare bosoms the steel-coats have fled,
Or, despite casque and corslet, lie dying and dead.

xi.

Brooke, Montague, Fleming, and Wingfield fled fast,
But the Queen's young O'Reilly hew'd round to the last:
To be nick-named Earl Cavan, Elizabeth's slave,
Struck Maolmora Breagh, sank the handsome and brave.

xii.

Not a tear for his fate, drop no dew on his corse!
The cravens were ill, but the traitor is worse;
The false to his country, the foe to his God,
Should have died on the scaffold, instead of the sod.

xiii.

And brave Harry Bagenal fell where he fought,
With many gay gallants—they slept as men ought:
Their faces to heaven—there were others, alack!
By pikes overtaken, and taken *aback*.

xiv.

And my Irish got clothing, coin, colours, great store,
Arms, forage, and provender—plunder *golòr;*
They munch'd the white manchets—they champ'd the
    brown chine,
Filleleu! for that day, how the natives did dine!

xv.

O'Nial looked on, when O'Shanaghan rose,
And cried, hearken Tyrone! I've a health to propose—
"To our Sassenach hosts!" and all quaff'd in huge glee,
With *Cead mile failte* got† BEAL-AN-ATH-BUIDH!

* *Up.*   † One hundred thousand welcomes to.

THE BURIAL OF ROLAND.

With balm, aloes, and myrrh, all was ended at eve,
   As Charlemagne gave us command;
Yet we linger'd around, for, ah! how could we leave
   What so late was—Roland.

On a gold-burnish'd bier, with rich silks overhung,
   Then we bore our lov'd County through Blaye;
And taper and torch, as his rest-hymn we sung,
   Kindled night into day!

And slow, and more slowly, we trode Saint Romaine
   Through a throng of the beanteous and brave,
A host of the living, who struggle and strain
   For one glance—at a grave.

Beneath the cuirass, who that caught the low moan,
   From bright eyes mark'd the fast falling tear,
Would have mated that moment a king on his throne,
   With Roland—on his bier!

Aye! proud were his obsequies, slain for our Lord,
   When Ronçevaux rang to the call
Of his clarion, and echoed the dints of his sword,
   Durandal, Durandal!

Oh! long shall the Saracen start at thy name!
   Dark ages its flashes illume;
Though our Emperor's seal to his Paladin's fame
   Be effaced from his tomb!

FROM THE FRENCH OF VICTOR HUGO.

O'er the water the moon sent a smile so serene!
  The casement at length is flung free to the breeze;
The Sultana looks forth, where dark islets are seen,
  With a fringe of white foam 'mid the silvery seas.

The lute from her fingers hath fallen, and hark!
  As it rings, comes a sound—had she heard it before
From the Greek Archipelago's deep-laden barque,
  Urged wearily on by the Ottoman oar?

Or while diving in turn, from the dusky sea-fowl,
  With pearls of the wave rolling over their wings?
Or some Djin, with a voice 'twixt a hiss and a growl,
  Who, in spite, the old stones off the battlement flings?

What noise dare ascend 'neath the harem's high wall,
  Save the cormorant's plunge, or old ocean's heart
    heaving,
Or a time-loosen'd stone from the tow'r, or the fall
  Of an interval oar, the blue Bosphorus cleaving?

Then whence that caique, and the boatmen who ply,
  A sack raised to the gunwale, then sunk; it is seen
To sway, as if—Allah!—a half-smother'd cry!
  O'er the water the moon sent a smile so serene!

THE PHILOSOPHER'S STONE.

The stone of the Philosopher in vain
I sought through many lands, with toil and pain;
Return'd, and found it—ah! why did I roam?
It was the hearthstone of my humble home!

THE SEAL,

FROM THE FRENCH OF BERANGER.

Thou gav'st this seal, where ivy seems to clip
  The elm, and say, I cannot live alone!
And Cupid, with a finger on his lip,
  Is deftly graven on the precious stone.
That seal is sacred, but it lends its aid,
  Alas! in vain, to keep a lover's vow;
Sophy, my pen is willing, but afraid—
  No secret, ev'n for love, no secret now!

" But why, when one brief line," wilt thou demand,
  " Would ease a heart that beats but for thy sake,
Why dost thou fear some enemy's rude hand,
  The little secret-guarding god should break ?"
I deem not the most jealous madman, dear,
  Would to his soul such infamy avow;
I shudder while I tell thee what I fear—
  No secret, ev'n for love, no secret now!

There is a reptile, Sophy, slimy, cold,
  Venice first found the venom of its stings;
With claws still clutching at the blood-bought gold;
  Hissing suspicion in the ears of kings;
It must see, read, know all, and all reveal!
  Must find, or make a crime no matter how;
It melts the wax, so easy to re-seal;
  No secret, ev'n for love, no secret now!

These words, sweet Sophy, traced for thee alone,
  That adder-eye, ere thine, hath noted well;
The tenderness thou only shouldst have known,
  May piece the newest plot, prepar'd to sell.

Perchance the raptures of a loving pair
  May smooth the wrinkles on a royal brow;
Despatch'd to court, to be derided there;
  No secret, ev'n for love, no secret now!

I fling away my pen; that balm, to heal
  The pangs of absence, fearfully I shun;
Why should I melt the wax, or stamp the seal?
  It will be broke, and Sophy be undone!
'Twas that *great* king, who La Valliére betray'd,
  Did with this dastard crime our France endow;
The curse of loving hearts upon his shade!
  No secret, ev'n for love, no secret now!

SONNET.

FROM THE ITALIAN.

To shun the flow'r, and to embrace the thorn;
  To leave all mirth, and live 'mid constant woes;
To choose a dungeon, whence there's no return;
  The ne'er re-op'ning gate, yourself to close;
To have your locks cut short like slaves we spurn,
  To cloud the light in each bright orb that glows;
Too late, within a convent, will you learn
  Those are the guerdons, and the glories those!
Maiden unwise, reflect, no further move;
  Some wayward vanity suggests a lot,
Which of those charms would rifle me and love.
  So spake the world; but ever to one spot
Her eye by faith unwav'ring fixed above,
  She heard the impious words as though she heard
    them not!

SONNET.

Oh, coffin not that form in cloister cold,
   Nor clip those love-locks fondled by the wind;
   Beauty's best office is to bless mankind,
And leave its type, when Death shall break the mould.
Then, fairest child, let home's pure pleasures hold
   On earth awhile, thy heav'n-aspiring mind;
   While infant arms thy neck shall gently bind,
Like roses round some ivory column roll'd.
So Nature spake; her pale cheek, yet more pale,
   While onward still, and upward bent her glance,
The Novice heard.   My mother will not fail
   In votaries, she said, more apt, perchance,
For these sweet duties; some may heav'nward sail,
While others row; enough, if both advance.

THE MINSTREL'S RETURN.

The Minstrel on his bier is lying,
   No song flows from his pallid lips;
And Daphne's yellow tresses, dying,
   Enwreath a brow in thought's eclipse.

They place the last lays of his singing,
   In richly-blazon'd scrolls around;
His lyre, of late so clearly ringing,
   Lies in his arms, and gives no sound!

So slumbers he the heavy slumber,
   While in each ear still breathes his lay,
And bitter thoughts each bosom cumber,
   As of a glory pass'd away.

Full many a month and year have vanish'd;
   Above his grave tall cypress glooms;
And those who wept when he seem'd banish'd,
   .Have sunk themselves in nameless tombs.

But as on earth Spring readvancing,
   Thrills strong emotion through all climes,
So ever-youthful, brightly glancing,
   The Minstrel comes to modern times.

For aye at one with life, a mirror,
   Not ev'n the Grave's dank breath can dim;
The age that thought him dead, strange error!
   Lives only in a Lay by Him!

ON WILHELM VON RODER.

LEFT ON THE FIELD AT KULM.

FROM THE GERMAN.

Perhaps a blither man than he
   To battle-field ne'er rode;
Nor one who yet more earnestly
   Had thought on Death, and God!

More fondly lov'd this world so fair,
   Or cherish'd child, and wife;
Or gave away as freely there,
   A Christian Hero's life!

God sent for him a message mild,
  And conquest on his crest,
Through sulph'rous mist the angel smil'd,
  And down he lay to rest.

Good night, dear Friend! none left below,
  Heav'ns denizen need weep;
Now ye who wake, charge home the foe,
  Your turn will come, to sleep!

WATERLOO.

FROM BERANGER.

Our vet'rans cried, we thank thy free-born muse,
  The nation's song can drown the nation's curse;
Laugh at the Bays a Faction would refuse,
  And give our gallant deeds another verse!
Sing us that day, despite its perfidy,
  Last of our fame though first of our decline:
I answer'd with a wet and downcast eye,
  Its name shall never sadden song of mine!

No Attic bard e'er breathes in music's tone
  Dire Chæronea's name; no Greek applauds,
While Athens, hurl'd by Fortune from her throne,
  And cursing Philip, doubts her idle gods!
Ev'n such a day hath seen our Empire fall,
  Seen strangers chain it to a hated line;
Hath seen, aye, Frenchmen! basely smile on all;
  Its name shall never sadden song of mine!

Perish the battle-giant! rise, rebel,
  Ye peoples, cried the pigmy-kings amain;
'Tis liberty that tolls his funeral-knell;
  Preserv'd by you, for you alone we reign!

The giant falls, and to enslave the earth
   Is since that day the ingrate Dwarfs' design,
That day of glory's death, not freedom's birth;
   Its name shall never sadden song of mine!

Lo! mortals of another age succeed,
   And wond'ring, turn, to ask me why I mourn?
And what is that sad wreck to them indeed,
   Since on the wave their cradles are upborne?
May they be happy! May their rising beam
   Efface that fatal Field's ill-omened shine!
Yet, though that day were but an empty dream,
   Its name shall never sadden song of mine!

Come children; on your foreheads let me read
   A future, bright with happiness and fame!
Your flashing eyes foretel the victor's meed,
   Oh haste to grow, and to rebuild our name!
For while of that dark day, when heav'n allowed
   Disaster's star to shed a ray malign,
While of that day remains the faintest cloud,
   Its name shall never sadden song of mine!

FROM THE GERMAN.

A lily shone in snowy white,
   The fair maid of the mountain;
Was ne'er so sweet a child of light
   By river, lake, or fountain.

Rush'd wild one eve the wind and rain,
   Till proudest trees bent under;
And black clouds lowr'd athwart the plain,
   Big with the brooding thunder.

And as I watch'd the far hill-side,
  The very earth seem'd shaking;
My lily-love, my beauteous bride;
  Thy tender stem is breaking!

From the swarthy cloud outflashed a line
  Of light, with ruddy quiver;
Oh lily, sweetest lily mine,
  Again I'll see thee, never!

I walk'd the wood all stript by storm,
  In summer's matin-hour;
And lo! my lily's lovely form,
  The queen of every flow'r.

The shatter'd rock lay bleak and bare,
  The stream o'er fragments flowing;
My lily smil'd, like a lassie there
  In joy, and beauty, blowing.

The glowing sun sprang glorious up,
  His golden arrows gleaming,
As they slanted off some tall tree-top,
  The first to hail his beaming.

And the grass was green in field and grove,
  That thunder-storm forgetting;
How fair will look my lily-love,
  When the level sun is setting!

For oh! her robe, so purely white
  Impearl'd with dew, shone clearly;
My flow'r, the moon's soft beam to-night
  Will match thy beauty dearly!

Night came; I sought my fav'rite spot,
  As the moon aloft was hieing;
But there I found my lily not,
  Nor drank her perfum'd sighing.

My lily-love, how low she lay!
  Her leaves all scath'd and scatter'd!
That Traitor Sun had kiss'd away,
  What Tempests had not shatter'd!

———

THE GRAVE.

FROM THE GERMAN.

The grave is deep and still;
  On its dark brink we stand,
And shudder at the vapors chill
  That veil the stranger-land!

The Nightingale's sweet call
  Thrills not its bosom cold;
Affection's roses only fall
  On heaps of mossy mould.

There vainly weep and wail
  Brides, early reft of bliss;
And piercing shrieks of orphans, fail
  To fathom that abyss!

No other house can sate
  Man's yearning after rest;
And only through this gloomy gate
  Wends homeward ev'ry guest.

L

The aching heart, down-weighed
With misery to the core,
Arrives at peace that cannot fade,
But when it beats no more!

————

SAME SUBJECT.

FROM THE GERMAN.

Life is such hot and heavy breath!
But light and cool the kiss of Death;
That kindly wafts us, where receives
Our quiet grave the wither'd leaves.

There falls the dew, the moonbeams smile,
As on the village-green the while;
And tears of Friendship softly gleam
In hope's mild onward-beck'ning beam.

Calm mother-earth collects us all
Within her lap, the great and small;
Oh! could we see our mother's face,
Tho' cold, how welcome her embrace!

————

THE IMAGINARY VOYAGE.

BERANGER.

Autumn flaps heavily his humid wing,
And brings me some new pang each lagging hour,
While sighing here, poor, weakly, nervous thing,
I watch the fall of pleasure's fading flow'r;

Oh! save me from Lutetia's marsh and mud;
  My lids might open to a sunny sky;
Bright dreams of Greece oft fir'd my youthful blood,
  'Tis there, 'tis there, I now would wish to die!

My Homer's French—the inference I scorn;
  Pythagoras is right; I was a Greek;
In time of Pericles, Athenian-born;
  And Socrates in prison lov'd to seek.
To Phidias' wonders incense wont to vow,
  'Mid flow'rs to watch Ilissus murmur bye,
I rous'd the bees upon Hymettus' brow,
  'Tis there, 'tis there, I now would wish to die!

Gods! let her genial sun a single day
  Dazzle mine eyes, but warm my wasted heart;
Hark! Freedom calls afar, Away, away!
  My Thrasybulus conquereth; depart!
Away! my barque is rocking off the strand,
  Kind Neptune, do not drown a summer fly!
Let my light Muse at the Piræus land,
  'Tis there, 'tis there, I now would love to die!

Oh, pure and mild, this soft Italian sky;
  But slav'ry all its azure doth obscure;
Away, my barque! on, on, and pass it bye,
  The day is dawning yonder, far more pure!
What waves are these, what rock that braves their roar
  What brilliant sun compels a downcast eye?
While tyranny expires upon the shore;
  'Tis there, 'tis there, that I would wish to die!

Athenian Virgins! deign to welcome here
  A poor Barbarian, as ashamed he sings;
For your *sweet* home he leaves a clime severe,
  Where wretched Genius is the slave of Kings.

Oh! save this lyre from tyranny malign,
  And should its chords awake one plaintive sigh,
Then, with Tyrtæus' ashes, mingle mine;
  To this fair land, I only come—to die!

ROSETTE.

FROM BERANGER.

Waste not those smiles, those tender tears,
  Wrong not your spring-time so,
While 'neath the load of forty years,
  My life is drooping low.
Yet once I felt love's flame; my belle
  An humble young coquette;
Ah! could I but love you as well
  As once I lov'd Rosette!

In splendid equipage and dress
  You drive, the Fashion's queen;
Rosette, though fresh and fair no less,
  Afoot was ever seen.
On others, too, her eyes would dwell,
  Then dance to see me fret;
    Ah, &c.

Your mirror'd boudoir, when you pass,
  Shows fifty beauteous faces;
Rosette had one small broken glass,
  I fancied it the Graces';
Around her couch no curtain fell,
  The morn's first glance she met;
    Ah, &c.

Your wit, were ev'n your beauty less,
   Would win the laurel meed;
And I must candidly confess
   Rosette could scarcely read;
But letters genius cannot spell,
   Young love by heart will get;
        Ah, &c.

With fewer charms, less frequent sighs,
   A heart less tender too,
At least, I never saw her eyes
   Look wistfully, like you;
Yet youth made all their arrows tell,
   My youth I but regret,
That never may I love as well
   As once I loved Rosette!

REMINISCENCES.

" Whom the gods love, die young."

Do you remember that bewitching girl,
   With lithesome shape, light step, and sunny smile,
And ruby lips half showing rows of pearl,
   And eyes that warmed the atmosphere, the while
'Twas perfumed by her breath, and pleasure spread
Round her, as from its centre—she is dead!

You may recal a rouged and wrinkled crone,
   Who said she'd been a beauty, and found few
That could believe her; she, who lived alone
   For slander, tea, vingt-un, or three-card loo;
Rich, yet too poor to lift the slightest ill
From earth-bow'd wretchedness—she's living still.

Do you remember an old palsied man,
　With one foot in the grave five years ago,
A bloated drunkard then; now, weak and wan,
　A driv'ling monument of vice and woe:
You must remember him; death seem'd t' arrive
Each morning at his door—he's still alive.

You recollect a fine, ambitious lad,
　Dark eyed, pale cheeked, who bore away each prize
At school and college, and who looked so sad
　The day he lost the fellowship; his eyes
Shone with strange light—they wanted rest, he said;
They had it, not long after—he is dead.

You knew a youthful mother, pure and sweet,
　As e'er was shrin'd a soul in human clay,
Whose children's eyes would ever turn to meet
　Their mother's, even in their wildest play;
You must have heard her doating husband vow
She was an angel—well, she may be, now.

God's ways are good; th' unlovely oft grow old;
　They yet may mend themselves, or warn their kind
And the warm eyes wax dim, the fond hearts cold,
　Reward, repose at least, they early find.
Man's longest day with all must swiftly end,
Let *us* do some small good ere night, dear friend.

ON THE DEATH OF A YOUNG GIRL.

FROM THE FRENCH.

Oh, why lament her youth,
　Or call death rough?
The gentle girl in sooth
　Was old enough.

Not the mere moments flown
  Ripen the pure;
The sinner's death alone
  Is premature.

SONNET.

Last night I stood within a mighty fane,
  Inscrib'd, the Temple of the Only God.
  Upon its solemn beauty, wrapt and aw'd,
I gaz'd, till its sublimity grew pain,
And made me sigh; when lo, the mystic chain
  That bound that lofty cupola and broad,
  Broke, and it fell away, like fragments flaw'd,
Dropping from some huge pearl, in lustrous rain.
But in its stead rose strangest shrines, alone
  In hideousness resembling, yet with look
Suiting each wild eidolon, by its own
  Fit votaries adored.   A sad voice spoke:
Man, which hath rear'd an altar, or a throne,
  On thy soul's ruins?   Groaning, I awoke.

1848.

The birth of another year, ghastly with graves,
For famine stalks on through the hovels of slaves;
A funeral wail!   But my heart feels so blank!
Slaves, fill me out wine, such as Thrasea drank,

When he and Helvidius, monarchs in worth,
Sate crown'd on the day that gave Brutus to earth.
Oh, those Romans of old, and this chain's weary clank!
Slaves, pour me out wine, such as Thrasea drank!

The torture of Tantalus, ever to read
Of Greece and of Rome; of the word and the deed;
High heaven! have *we* souls, among men do *we* rank?
Slaves, lavish such liquor as Thrasea drank;

In a bowl of beechwood, or my land's kindly clay,
Men are starving, hence, goblet of silver, away!
There were blood on your brim, there were tears in the
    draught,
Slaves, crown it with wine, such as Thrasea quaff'd.

Bead the bowl, fill it high, higher, up with it yet!
He drank to remember, I drink to forget;
We have crouch'd to be famish'd; at insult have
    laugh'd.
Slaves! this is not wine such as Thrasea quaff'd.

The wine, ah, what was it; the thoughts it inspir'd,
Proud mem'ries it woke, and high hopes which it fir'd,
Freedom's smile over all; in each heart how it sank!
Slaves! ye have no wine such as Thrasea drank!

EPIGRAM.

A rhymer, by another badly treated,
    Penn'd a long satire, venom to the brim,
And then o'er me the whole of it repeated;
    But I had never injured him.

BALLAD.

FROM LORD HOLLAND'S LIFE OF LOPE DE VEGA,
VOL. I. PAGE 71.

Thrice the sun had sank and mounted
    Since the crowning of the king,
And Count Villa Mediana
    Sparkled in the courtly ring,

As 'mid duller gems the diamond,
  When a shape to mirth a stranger,
Cross'd him like a gloomy shadow,
  Said—Beware! your life's in danger.

Uncle of Duke Olivarez,
  Thy confessor gave the warning,
But the Count, so wild and haughty,
  Paid him back with scoff and scorning.

Bird of darkness, keep thy croaking
  For my foe, he answered proudly;
Thou the raven, he the craven,
  Flock together—laugh'd then loudly.

And that ev'ning, on the Prado,
  Was a low voice heard to say,
Stop, Count Villa Mediana!
  Hearken, what brooks no delay!

Scarcely sprang he from the carriage,
  When his bosom sheath'd a dagger;
Vainly sought his hand the sword-hilt,
  Down he fell in one wild stagger.

Why died Villa Mediana?
  I have mention'd where and how;
More inquiry then made no man,
  More can any answer now?

Nay, why not? what sin concealer,
  E'er could hope to baffle Time,
That sure sleuth-hound, the revealer,
  Here or yonder scenting crime?

Why died Villa Mediana?
  For his galling tongue, or pen,
From the rage of jealous women,
  Or revenge of injur'd men?

For his jibes, that stung the wittols,
  Arts, that made their dames disloyal?
Both, perchance, but black suspicion,
  Broods o'er names no less than royal.

For 'tis whisper'd, Philip, winding
  Through a passage of the palace,
Stole behind the queen, and blinding
  Her bright orbs in sport or malice,

Suddenly she cried unguarded,
  Count, what would you? down the king
Dropp'd his hands, and eyed in silence,
  Her, who pale and quivering,

Stood a moment, then said smiling,
  Count of Barcelona,* wherefore
Take such pleasure in beguiling
  Ladies, you no longer care for?

And the king responded, only
  With a hollow sort of laughter;
But Count Villa Mediana
  Somehow did not live long after.

ON A BEE.

CONCETTO OF MAFFEI BARBARINI, (POPE URBAN VIII.)

Lo! not for sweets alone doth roam,
Yon cunning builder of the comb;
  His wax, when day is done,
Will light up many a happy home,
Religious fane, and regal dome,
  Small rival of the sun!

* A Title of the Kings of Spain.

FROM THE GERMAN OF HENRICH HEINE.

I lay and slept from anguish free,
　For it had ceas'd, afraid
Of a mute form, that seem'd to me
　Earth's most angelic maid.

Pale as the pure Carrara stone,
　She stole all stilly there,
With pearly eyne, while black roll'd down
　Like thunder-clouds her hair.

And softly, softly, floated nigh
　The marble-pallid maid,
Till on the couch I felt her lie,
　Where, wond'ring, I was laid.

I felt her kiss, I felt above
　Her bosom of the snow;
I seem'd enrapt with awe and love,
　And full of joy and woe.

How quivers, pants, my longing heart,
　And throbs, and burns so bold!
But, ah! no warmth can I impart
　To one so icy cold!

My bosom may not move, nor beat;
　Cold ever, icy cold,
Yet tho' without love's genial heat,
　His sway I share of old.

On lip and cheek no blush may glow,
　My heart may run no blood;
Yet writhe not, strive not, mortal, so,
　Am I not kind and good?

She clasp'd me closer; ah! I fear'd
  My life about to fail!
When crow'd the cock, and disappear'd
  The maiden, marble pale!

———

THE ANGEL'S KISS.

VERSIFIED FROM THE GERMAN.

Beatrice, having caused a young friend, Rosalia, to faint by
representing an angel, stooping to kiss her, in a religious
ceremony, fancies she has killed her, leaves her home in a state
of distraction, and flies to Rome. Poverty compels her at first
to become a model for artists, and subsequently the mistress
of a wealthy Russian, for whom she does not feel or feign the
slightest affection. A former German lover and Rosalia, find
her at length as described. She has acted throughout under
a kind of monomania, that her degradation is an atonement
for what she considers, though an involuntary act, a murder.
Hence her despair at seeing Rosalia alive, and finding that her
sacrifice of every blessing connected with home, friends, and
lover, and even of her delicacy and chastity was wholly vain.

'Twas a high festival, when thousands come
In hope to find the road to heav'n, through Rome:
'Neath an old arch, beside a ruin'd wall
Sate Beatrice; at a glance I saw it all.
Her so-call'd lover then had sought his home,
That she amid the world's bleak waste might roam
What could it matter? She look'd pale, thin, ill;
And neither sang, nor pray'd, but sate quite still,
Save that she sometimes folded, as for pray'r,
A baby's hands whom in her lap she bare,
As if she thought a hope to be forgiv'n
Lay only in that young thing's signs to heav'n.
We came upon her suddenly; her eyes
Dilated; but of terror or surprise,

Was little trace in gesture or in hue,
And yet her poor wan face more rigid grew,
And her slight form seem'd stiff'ning into stone,
While gazing on Rosalia, who had grown
Taller no doubt, with more luxuriant hair,
But the same silver bodkin fasten'd there,
Her garb the same—the same calm angel air.
It is no spirit then! so might I trace
The breaking of the spell on Beatrice' face;
Then rush'd a tide of crimson o'er her cheek,
Her brow, her bosom; what doth it bespeak?
Love, gratitude? ah, no! deep pain, and hate,
And frenzy at the thought, too late! too late!
She sprang up wildly, glar'd around, below;
Stoop'd, clutch'd a heavy stone, but trembled so,
She could not raise it; then she grasp'd the boy
To dash him at Rosalia, and destroy
Both at one blow; her body was too weak,
And sank upon its knees; she could not speak,
But knelt, the babe before her, while her breath
Came in the short deep gasps that pant for death,
And shiver'd, as beneath some glacier's chill,
With the heart's deadly cold, despair; until
Her small teeth chatter'd, and I saw too well
Her bosom torn with torments, as of hell;
For when Rosalia stoop'd, and would have press'd
Her wretched friend to her all-loving breast,
She thrust her back with passionate disdain,
Yea, snatch'd the hand that sued for her's in vain,
And gnash'd her teeth upon it; Rosalia
Drew it not back, whate'er the pain might be,
With pity smil'd, and bore it patiently.
Poor Beatrice! That slow-fading torture flush,
Some might have fancied beauty's conscious blush,
A beauty far surpassing earthly charms,
As thro' her dark hair gleam'd her snowy arms,

And her face bore a meek and heav'nly cast,
And grew still fair, and fairer to the last.
Yet when Rosalia cried, I live, I live,
She falter'd, Hush!   I cannot yet forgive!
Look there, Rosalia, make that babe unborn,
Make me as pure as on the fatal morn
When my kiss kill'd thee; I will bless thee then;
But else, avoid me, go; nor come again
Within mine eyes; for death is on me now;
And it is very bitter; do not thou
Increase my agony; she heard her call,
And turn'd her face a little to the wall,
And motion'd us away; the sun by chance
Then setting, sent a soften'd parting glance
Upon those closing orbs; they op'd, to see
Rosalia, yet again; then turn'd to me;
And death had kindly conquer'd ev'ry feeling
Except of love, ere yet those sweet lids sealing,
And when she sought her child, the failing gleams
Strove to meet mine; I see them in my dreams!
Each press'd a hand, that lay in ours, too weak
To press again; the angel kiss'd her cheek,
A gasp or twain—and then the broken-hearted
Slept well, and our poor lost one had departed.
And my coy sisters need no more cry shame!
My mother wish no more, she could not blame,
My friends feel awkward, when a child they see
Clasp'd to the breast, or clinging to the knee,
Of one ne'er wedded, and who ne'er will be!

SLAVERY.

A crash in the distance; say what may it mean,
That the cheek of the pale-face looks paler, I ween?
The clashing of chains? what wild fancies are these
'Tis the rattle of sugar-canes sway'd by the breeze.

The planter's young wife in the fast-falling gloom,
Sits alone; but, ha! is she alone in that room?
Then why stops the pulse of the planter's young bride?
She feels that some being is close at her side!

How noiseless his tread! cat or camel alone,
With their cushion-clad feet may as stilly steal on;
And the pearly-white eyne, and his teeths' ghastly gleam';
She shudders, and scarcely represses a scream.

And where is her husband? Oh, misery, shame!
In the hut of that slave, who so noiselessly came;
And what doth he there? Will he tell his young wife?
Ah! the slave casts a shadow that darkens her life.

If that be a life, which is measur'd by fears,
By jealousy, trembling, repining, and tears;
Far better be dead—there is rest in the grave,
Than to gasp out existence, the slave of a slave!

FROM UHLAND.

Look up; see where angels have borne thy dear brother,
  Because he ne'er vex'd me—look Wilhelm, I say!
Then tell me how I may most teaze you, dear mother,
  Or some angel may take me away.

TO THE HORSES OF AURORA.

Ye cloud-fleck'd coursers of the dawn,
  That o'er yon level paw, and play,
Ere wimpled night hath all withdrawn,
  To clear the verge of day.

Oh, happy steeds, besprent with dew,
  And harness'd by the laughing Hours,
While Hope and Hebe flatter you,
  And fret each mane with flow'rs.

Yours is the pure and primal charm,
  The conscious smile of mother earth,
To see her renovated form,
  And beauty's latest birth.

Yours is the matin-song of birds,
  The virgin-blossom's rathest scent;
The babbling infant's half-form'd words,
  The insect's merriment.

Oh, happy steeds, your task is done
  Before the day-god mounts his car;
His hot and weary wheels drag on,
  But ye are sped afar.

Say, ever-young, where is your home,
  In rustling groves, or dewy dells,
Or do ye roam by ocean foam
  O'er variegated shells?

In shady grotto, of some sphere
  Beyond our ken, do ye abide?
Aurora tossing nightly near
  By old Tithonus' side.

There, with low neighings, oft ye own
  Her cool caressing finger-tips,
And quaff the fragrance freshly blown
  From her rich ruddy lips!

Light-stepping steeds, of dappled gray,
  Though welcome now to none, or few,
When innocent, and kind, and gay,
  Man lov'd to look on you!

For you the shepherd tun'd his pipe,
  The hunter wound his cheerful horn,
And all on earth was ready-ripe
  To hail the car of morn.

But now, alas, how changed of cheer,
  Lorn labour of his rest ye spoil,
And waken to a world so drear,
  Of want, and woe, and toil.

The haggard factory child ye blight,
  Who learns so soon that sleep's a crime;
And starting up at dead of night,
  Cries, *father*,* is it time?

While luxury shuts out the dyes
  Ye herald o'er the cob-web'd lawn,
And perishes before his eyes
  Have ever dar'd the dawn.

Live arrows from Apollo's bow,
  Heralds of day, triumphant team,
How must ye snort to see below
  A world of gas and steam,

Where Phœbus, Venus, Muse, and Grace,
  Are only idle words of old;
And all earth's ancient gods give place
  To Mammon's throne of gold.

* Fact; as Miss Edgeworth says. The poor little girl had,
vbably, no Mother.

M.

"AS FAIR AS LADY DONE."

IMITATION OF THE LAKE STYLE.

Just where an humble cottage show'd
    Beneath an old oak tree,
A woman sate beside the road,
With a small babe that chirp'd and crow'd,
    And laugh'd right lustily.

She dandled it upon her knee,
    Then lifted it to the sun,
And cried, Before thou settest, see
The fairest lass; aye, is not she
    As fair as Lady Done?

And who is Lady Done, I said,
    That is so wonder-fair;
The youthful mother shook her head,
I wot not, sir; where I was bred,
    'Tis just a saying there.

This saying, as I jogged along,
    Began my wits to probe,
Recall'd the wealthy, patient, strong,
Of classic lore and sacred song,
    Hercules, Crœsus, Job.

What are they now, the fam'd of yore?
    All but a name is gone,
With some, "as this," "as that," before;
And what is Helen's glory more
    Than, "Fair as Lady Done."

THE ROBIN.

LAKE STYLE.

When I am sullen—call it, sad—
  I seek the garden near;
Where trees in fading colours clad,
  Bespeak the jaundiced year,
I hear a flutter quick and glad—
  An undersong I hear—
        It is the robin.
He recks not of my knitted brow,
Nor need—it glooms no longer now.
        Good morrow, robin!

How beautiful, I ne'er can say
  When tuneless people sing;
'Twere better they were taught to pray,
  Or preach—or, anything;
And, yet, for one who sings to-day
  My rugged rhymes I string,
        With, bravo! robin.
He seems to hear my praise with pride,
And cocks his little pate aside,
        The funny robin.

Then hops and croons between my feet;
  I rest upon my spade,
And say, how sweet, encore, how sweet,
  You saucy little blade!
And who then flirts away so fleet,
  Pretending he's afraid—
        It is the robin;
Then gulps a grub right greedily,
And carols for himself and me,
        The reckless robin.

He follows to the cherry tree,
  And there we sit, and peer
In one another's eyes. I see
  All faith in his, no fear.
That small fowl much hath solaced me,
  By venturing so near.
          And now, the robin,
Thinks my straw hat a roost for him,
And, winking, perches on its rim.
          Cool, master robin!

Should not man thus all fortune own,
  Follow where it may lead;
Aye, tho' his brighter hopes be flown,
  His heart beat, but to bleed;
Its ruddy mark need not be shown,
  For every one to read,
          Like ensign robin's.
Then let the real red-cross knight
Wear his within, but dare the fight,
          Like bold cock-robin.

FROM VICTOR HUGO.

One day Ali passed bye, and the haughtiest crown
To his Arnaout's high stirrups its turban bent down,
  And the mob shouted, Allah! and bless'd him;
When a dervise, so old, blood scarce flow'd in his veins,
Cleft his way through the throng, caught his horse by
  the reins,
  And thus he address'd him:

"Ali Tepeleni, thou light, thou sun-burst,
Who in the divan sittest highest, and first,
    Whose great name is aye growing greater;
Thou visier, with such numberless warriors array'd,
Thou shade of the Shah, of great Allah the shade,
    Thou'rt a dog, and a traitor!

"A glare from the grave lights thee on, thou unknowing,
Thy wrath's like a cup that is fill'd to o'erflowing,
    Thy friends, as thy foes, find no quarter;
Thy crescent shines here, like a sickle in wheat,
And thou grindest, to make thy proud palace complete,
    Bones in blood for the mortar!

" But thy day will soon come; Janina will find room
'Mid her fast-crumbling ruins for thee and thy tomb,
    And God keeps a necklace of iron
For thee, 'neath the tree where the shivering souls
Of the impious load all the black branches in shoals,
    And which hell's sev'nfold night doth environ.

" A demon shall read from a blood-inscribed roll,
Thy victims' long list to thy shuddering soul,
    While thou viewest around by strange glamour
The empty-vein'd spectres, all streak'd with their gore,
Passing numberless bye, and more coming, and more
    Than the accents thy terror would stammer.

" Thy fort with its cannon, thy fleet with its speed,
Shall not aid thee a whit in thine uttermost need;
    No fighting for thee, and no flying,
Though Ali Pacha, like the filthy Jew, lie,
And to cheat the dark angel, who watches hard bye,
    Take a false name, when dying!"

'Neath his costly pelisse, Ali wore a poignard,
A crater-mouth'd carabine, sharp scymitar,
    And three horse-pistols, loaded for service.
He heard the old man, spoke no word all the while;
Bent his head, as in thought, and then flung, with a smile,
    His pelisse to that plain-spoken dervise.

ON RETSCH'S GAME OF CHESS.

The game is open'd—not a game for those
Who seek from wearing work a brief repose,
Nor yet for parents, happy 'mid the noise
Of romping girls, and never-resting boys;
No play for youth and beauty, where is heard
Nor lightsome laugh, nor gay nor tender word.
Grave, silent game, at which ev'n fools look wise,
And dearest friends feel much like enemies.
What is it here then, where the very room
Shows like a vault, the table is a tomb,
The playmen, passions; and oh, fearful odds,
No adversaries less than fallen gods!
Man's soul the stake for which such pow'rs contend,
The game is opened; oh, how will it end?
Mark well the players: on the left is one
A pure eye doth not love to look upon,
Yet feels the fascination of the snake,
Like the poor bird that flutters in the brake.
The lip compress'd and cold; the eye severe;
The dev'lish smile that curdles to a sneer;
The threadbare courtesy that chills the good,
Put on, to cloak a wolfish thirst for blood;
The features, fine but haggard; fingers thin,
Like talons, ever clutching what they win;
All, all pourtray the great arch-gamester well,
Who play'd so false in heav'n, and won a hell.

And who his rival? is that slight fair youth
With lip of innocence, and eye of truth,
Whose thoughts lie clear as pebbles in a brook,
We read them in each lineament and look;
Is he to play against the prince of air,
The sire of lies, the serpent, the soul slay'r?
Ah, vain the struggle, tho' beside him still
A Seraph-shape, to him invisible,
Watches and lingers, like some drooping dove,
That shivers, yearns, but cannot save its love.
Such are the forms that deep attention claim,
Hush, hold your breath, and watch that awful game.
Lo Pleasure, Satan's queen, to lure man's soul
Bares her white bosom, brims her sparkling bowl;
His peace is lost, his pray'rs begin to fail,
Sloth cumbers him, and scorpion doubts assail;
But Hope remains to cheer the desolate,
And some pure aspirations to heaven's gate,
And man, tho' Love is lost, hath vanquish'd Hate;
While Faith, his queen, upholds the cross divine,
Oh Father, may he conquer in that sign!
Satan hath won from him both Peace and Love,
Yet cannot cloud the day-spring from above;
But man must lose the game, he must—'tis clear;
Nay, prophecy were but presumption, here.

Behold yon sinless suff'rer! anguish now
Extorts a ruddy dew from that pale brow;
Oh hear him fervently, but vainly, pray
For this last bitter cup to pass away;
Nail'd to the cross then sigh his soul abroad,
Oh why forsake me thus, my God, my God!
Who could have fancied in His last faint breath
The death, that was to conquer time and death!
Then *say not* man must lose; a higher pow'r
Contends with evil; tho' its clouds may low'r

They cannot last, before the coming day,
When doubt and darkness breaking melt away;
And Faith, full plum'd to knowledge, then can show
How one false move endanger'd all below,
While hope, as but a milder form of fear,
Expires in smiles, 'mid love's eternal year.

FROM THE FRENCH OF BERNARD.

Let other Damons curse or bless
  The beauty of some Goddess;
My flame is but a Shepherdess,
  Who wears a simple boddice.
I sang a hundred hymns to Love,
  His praise my joy and duty,
And gain'd his gratitude to prove,
  This master-piece of beauty.

Of Dora's ancestors I find
  Not e'en the smallest traces;
Her gestures prove her in my mind,
  A sister of the Graces;
Within her breast warm feelings reign,
  It owns not sect, nor system,
And had Sir Isaac been her swain,
  I doubt if she'd have kiss'd him.

Yet oft a sigh, a look or kiss,
  Form all our conversation;
My constant study but her bliss,
  My pleasure, her vocation;
Hers is the true magnetic eye
  That takes and keeps possession,
Her voice a modulated sigh,
  Yet rich with one expression.

Her rosy hue is all her own,
   Fond zephyr's search beguiling;
Her face a rose-bud newly blown,
   That blossoms in her smiling;
A lilac sprig is all her pride,
   When at her simple toilet;
I fancy ev'n the flowers that hide
   Her figure—only spoil it.

Two feelings seem to sway her breast;
   That wave of summer ocean
Now sinks, with modesty opprest,
   Then heaves with warm emotion;
Her eyes contain a magic fire,
   Her purity impedes it,
By turns the flashing of desire,
   The languor that succeeds it.

My Dora joins to all her charms,
   A shape divinely moulded,
Which seems to ask her Lover's arms
   Each moment to enfold it;
Such are her traits; it is above
   My art to add another;
Yet stay; she is the age of Love,
   The image of his mother.

LINES WRITTEN AT ANTWERP, IN THE CHARACTER OF A CATHOLIC.

Do Englishmen deem ought Divine?
   The Holy Font they saunter bye,
They bend no knee, and make no sign,
   But gaze with cold or curious eye

On Him who came for man to die,
  And on his people kneeling there,
Who o'er their sins remorseful sigh,
  Or pour their souls in pious pray'r.

And when as connoisseurs they scan
  The Form that none should view unaw'd,
It is to praise the skill of Man,
  But not to bless the love of God.
Ah, not like Him to kiss the rod,
  To drain the bitter cup they came,
To spread a Father's name abroad;
  No! Rubens is their Idol's name!

Yet these be men who cannot pray
  Save in some meanly barb'rous pile;
The Heart is all in all, they say,
  And look superior the while;
Have we no hearts, or hearts of guile,
  Which offer all that Genius grac'd,
And doth Heav'n deign alone to smile
  On emblems of the vilest taste?

We will not worship in their barns
  Nor learn their cold, or stolen prayers;
We will not change a Faith that warns,
  Yet cheers and purifies, for theirs!
We will transmit it to our heirs,
  As we received it—on a Rock—
And see each Sect that madly dares
  Collision—perish by the shock!

HYMN.

Faint, as the first pale streaks of morn,
  The dayspring's doubtful light,
That wakes a hope in hearts new-born
  To shake off Sin and Night.

And deadly cold the spirit feels,
  Ere troubled thoughts unroll,
And that glad Message gently steals
  To renovate the soul.

Despair not, child of earth, press on!
  Now is the time to pray;
'Tis ever colder just ere dawn,
  And darker, ere the day.

An ear is open to thy cry,
  To heaven's sure promise cling,
For grace to clear the clouded eye,
  And thaw the frozen spring.

Take up thy cross, and gladly bear,
  And patient kiss the rod;
So may that trembling dawn of pray'r
  Precede the Noon of God!

THE AMAZON.

Lo, where the Amazon with anxious eye,
  But steadfast arm, poises the thirsty lance!
Not all unaw'd at brute ferocity,
  Scorn mantling o'er her fair stern countenance,

She scans the Leopard, as St. Michael's glance
  The Adversary—not so doom'd to die !
And tho' her gen'rous charger's pangs enhance
  Our sympathy, she hath no breast to sigh.
Type of a war beyond Homeric song,
  Above all Roman, Saracen, or Hun ;
War with our brutal passions—oh, how long
  Till that great spirit combat be begun,
And upborne by opinion, swift and strong,
  Each glorious woman prove an Amazon !

FAIR SUE.

FROM GERMAN OF BURGER.

Fair Sue my neighbour long had been,
  A gentle girl was Sue,
And one could spy with half an eye
  Kind, good and modest too.
I went and came, I came and went
  So ebbs and flows the sea ;
I met her still with merriment,
  And left her fain and free.

At length I found, poor simple lad,
  A change within my heart,
I flew to meet her still, so glad,
  But went, how loath to part !
No other pastime first could please,
  My business then she grew,
Until my life by soft degrees,
  Was all absorb'd in Sue.

My senses next resign'd their pow'r,
  My voice had lost its tone;
For me there bloom'd nor leaf, nor flow'r,
  But Susan bloom'd alone.
The sun and moon, and starry skies,
  That Girl so fill'd my mind,
I saw their light but in her eyes,
  And star'd myself stark blind.

And yet within a little space
  Quite chang'd my feelings grew,
Tho' sense and beauty, wit and grace,
  Remain'd the while in Sue.
I went and came, I came and went,
  So ebbs and flows the sea,
I met her only with content,
  And left her sorrow-free.

Ye Sages, who have time to spare,
  Who can so clearly prove
How, when and where all creatures pair,
  And why we kiss and love;
Philosophers! oh tell me now,
  With solemn saw and face,
The secret springs, why, when, and how,
  Of this mysterious case!

I muse myself both night and day,
  Again all day and night,
On these strange things—yet cannot say
  I yet read aught aright.
For love is like the ocean-wind,
  It breathes upon our hearts;
But whence it cometh can we find,
  Or whither it departs?

LOVE'S OMNIPRESENCE.

FROM THE FRENCH.

Where most—one day ask'd Fanny fair,
. Doth Love delight to roam?
Said I, his empire's ev'rywhere,
And ev'rywhere his home.
He opens from Aurora's car
The portals of each day,
And in his hue yon sun afar
Mounts, glows, and glides away.

All nature owns his balmy kiss,
With yonder lamb he springs,
He murmurs in each brook of bliss,
Or with the warbler sings.
With each sweet simple violet
He hides in grassy sod;
And in her flutterfly's fine net,
The girl hath caught—a god!

He breathes from ev'ry flow'r that blows,
Is seen in ev'ry bloom;
'Tis he who gives this budding rose
Such beauty, and perfume;
But when disdaining meaner lures,
He feeds on lovers' sighs,
Sweet Fan, he wears that form of yours,
And dazzles in its eyes.

SONNET.*

ON THE LIKENESS OF A BOY SHOOTING AT A TARGET.

What heart hath never sigh'd, ah, Time, restore
  My childhood's merry laugh, the violet smell
  Spring used to waft, and tints too fair to dwell
Beyond the dawn.   Fond memory loves to pore
On fleeting forms, like Egypt's sons of yore
  Embalming the departed ; yea, the spell
  Of Art, her wond'rous handmaid doth compel
The bloom to pause upon the flow'r, before
It fades or ripens into graver hues ;
  And thus we see young Eros' counterpart
  Smiling triumphant that his arrow told ;
Oh ! centre thus each aim on Virtue's gold,
And seldom tears those laughing eyes suffuse,
  And late, beloved, own a surer dart !

FROM THE FRENCH.

When the friend becomes the lover,
  All the peace of life is gone :
Cares around us ever hover
When the friend becomes the lover,
Newer stings we still discover :
  Wake at night ; by day look wan ;
When the friend becomes the lover,
  All the peace of life is gone.

* This Sonnet had at least the merit of suggesting those of my
Brother.   It was suggested by a likeness of the eldest son of my
friend, Dr. Anster, by Burton.

When the lover turns a friend,
　　All the charm of life is past,
Oh, the scentless vapid end,
When the lover turns a friend !
Though esteem's pale orb ascend,
　　Ah ! the sun is setting fast:
When the lover turns a friend,
　　All our golden prime is past !

XIXth SONNET OF PETRARCH.

The nearer I approach the sure release
　　Of the last day that limits mortal woe,
　　I find Time's rapid current faster flow,
And my delusive hopes from it decrease.
Then to my thoughts I say, we soon shall cease
　　Converse on love : this earthly load, although
　　Both hard and heavy, passeth like the snow
Of yesterday, and we shall be at peace.
　　For with it down will topple ev'ry hope,
That made us dote on vanity so long,
　　With smile and tear, with terror and disdain;
Then shall we clearly see, how through this throng
　　Of things perplexing, some will find free scope,
While others sigh so often, and in vain !

RONDEAU,

FROM CLEMENT MAROT.

I' the good old times, a love-tale might be told
Without much art, and heard without much gold ;
　　So that a nosegay, if love nestled there,
　　Was guerdon rich as the round earth could bear,

When only on the heart was sought a hold.
Did some perchance their ladye-loves enfold,
Wot ye how long they cherish'd, nor grew cold,
   Twenty—aye thirty years, a love affair,
                   'I the good old times !

But now-a-days, hearts would seem lost, unsold ;
Feign'd tears, caprice alone we now behold,
   Wherefore who'd have me much for love to care,
   Must find it first, and for the better wear,
Recast it in th' unfashionable mould,
                  O' the good old times !

THE NEGRO'S ESCAPE.

Night came : the Negro strain'd his wistful sight
   Round fields where once his childhood lov'd to roam ;
   Then plung'd beneath the dark wood's welcome dome,
And sped on hastily, till dawning light
Disclos'd an humble dwelling, with a slight
   Mark on the door-post : when his breath could come,
   He tapp'd, and ask'd, Is this the Wand'rer's Home ?
The bolt shot back, and a kind voice said, Right !
   Its farewell tones were, Follow the North Star !
     And oft return'd those words as over broad
Savannahs, on, from fetter, lash, and scar
   It beckon'd, that bright, holy thing afar !
His joy-thrill'd spirit oft it sooth'd, and awed,
In after-life; to him, the eye of God !

                        N

ON A PORTRAIT OF SARSFIELD.

Brave Sarsfield, thy likeness is hanging above,
A breast full of daring, a face full of love;
And over thine armour, strange contrast of grace,
Softly mingled with sternness! depends the rich lace;
There are coronet, cuirass, and famed fleur de luce,
And for crest, an arm sworded in deadliest use;
Wild shamrock and bay-leaves, a garland so meet,
And two tall Irish Staghounds repose at thy feet.
"The stout Sarsfield" thy title; thy slogan too, there,
Is "Mary with us and St. Bride of Kildare"!
As I've looked on that portrait, how oft have I felt,
What a blending of blood and of milk in the Celt!
So cunning, so simple; ferocious, and mild;
A warrior, a woman, a savage, a child.
The attributes here seem as oddly allied,
The Virgin and battle, grim war and St. Bride;
A helm wreath'd with flow'rs like a death's head with
     pearls,
Arms forg'd by swart men, woven lace of fair girls;
Ev'n the deer-hounds, with sinews relaxed, seem to nap,
Like Samson reposing in Dalilah's lap,
Such may image stout Sarsfield in peace and in war;
But at Landon struck down, from his country afar,
No hero of Greece, and no champion of Rome,
Surpass'd his last words as he thought of his home!
His death wound he clutched with a hand dripping red
In his lifeblood, alas, for the foreigner shed:
Then held it aloft, while the red dew down fell,
Amid thoughts of the land he had loved long and well;
"Oh, that this were for Ireland!" the patriot cried;
Those words will live long, though the warrior died.

DERMOT M'MORROGH.

He died at Ferns—his name his testament:
Unhousel'd, unaneal'd, impenitent,
Without confession, or absolving prayer,
Worm-eaten, conscience-stricken, in despair;
Dermot, a traitor ever, erst a king,
Who two years syne the Norman horde did bring
To waste his native land, and then unaw'd
And tir'd of slaying men, attack'd ev'n God
Thro' his pure saints, Finan, and Columcill,
Burned down their churches, at his impious will,
Profan'd their sacred shrines at Kells, Clonard,
And warr'd on heav'n, as tho' on earth he warr'd.
Two years this lasted; no eclipse, no storm,
No thunder spake, but lo, th' avenging worm
Swarm'd in his breathing carcase, which became
Loathsome and rotten as the hated name
He left behind; oh, ponder on his doom!
Alive to feel the fretters of the tomb,
Yet dread to die, for darkling he sees still
Thy frown St. Finan, thine, St. Columcill!
Dearvorghal here, there injured Tiarnan stands,
Shudd'ring he veils his eyes with nerveless hands,
But shuts not out his people's curse and groan
Appealing vainly to a heart of stone:
Hating and hated in his living grave,
Without one hope to shelter or to save,
What boots him now his rude barbarian strength,
His deep hoarse voice, and limbs of sinewy length?
The heart that knew nor pity. love, nor fear?
All force of man, alas, how feeble here!
So ling'ring dies M'Morrogh, feeling well
Life's long dark vista ends in flames of Hell!
And leaves no blacker traitor to record,
Since that dread night when Judas sold his Lord.

RONDEAU.

FROM THE FRENCH.

(To a friend inquiring if I remembered the first avowal of love.)

If I remember that delicious hour,
  When he, my husband now, beside me stood;
Not half so fair methinks, the regal flow'r
  The half-blown rose by Zephyr softly wooed,
While Philomel, leaf-hidden, charms the bower.
  When thus he whispers, shall no richer dower
Reward my pain than cold ingratitude?
  Ah, cruel one, to ask while my tears shower,
                      If I remember!

Learn, then, that while with love and fear I cower,
  He cries, Thou must be mine, proud-hearted prude!
And kisses, everywhere, until all power
  Failing, I die in his embrace so rude;
How then can I remember, of that hour
                      If I remember?

THE BUCANEER'S BRIDAL.

What thou hast been I know not, nor ask whence thou
    art;
Thou scarce hadst been here, if in any one's heart;
I question thee not if thy life were unblam'd,
Thou wert nothing to me; why should I be asham'd?
To others, perchance, there were wrongs to atone,
Or to thine own breast, when thy will was thine own.
Pledge thyself for the future, thou'rt quit of the past,
Mine now, whatsoever, whosever thou wast;
Thou hast now one to love, and it may be, to fear;
Thou art bride of a true and a bold Bucaneer!

Now hearken ! his musket he struck till it rang
On the rock, and the woman was chill'd with the clang;
If falsehood henceforward should sully thy name,
Here's one who hath ever been true to my aim ;
She's here at our bridal, will doom our divorce,
Thou'rt mine for the better, and her's for the worse !
No altar or priest, no gold circle, sweet token,
Their hands bound in one, yet the pledge was unbroken;
May St. Marie-la-bonne, a troth-plight never hear,
Worse kept than the bride's of that wild Bucaneer !

For his barque sank at sea ; and deserted, his band ;
And the brown Bess he trusted so, burst in his hand ;
His horse flung the rider, while short snapt the rein,
And he lay, fever raging in every vein,
Forsaken and wounded, and burning with thirst,
Till in his despair he'd have prayed—as he curs'd ;
Alone? not alone—for long sought, found at last,
His forehead was bath'd, and white lips till he pass'd ;
He was kiss'd, he was sooth'd in his anguish and fear,
Then sank, none to aid, thy lorn bride, Bucaneer !

FAIRY TALE.

A lord of Argouges, who once liv'd near Bayeux,
(But how near I don't know, so I cannot tell you)
  Was belov'd by a Fairy
  Of wond'rous renown
  In that region and town :
The name of that beauty so airy,
She had not been christen'd, like Bessie or Mary,
To these days has never come down.

But the knight, her pet client,
  (In love, not in law,)
  By her aid stood in awe
Of no dragon, magician, or giant,
Who cut but poor figures
  When he took delight,
  And quite as a right,
  To wallop them well,
  Should they dare to rebel,
As Americans wallop their niggers.
At last his aerial houri
  Grew so fond of the knight, that she led
    A very dull life when away
  From her hero the length of a day,
And so the lov'd mortal she wed,
And brought him a very large dowry.
When love is the only solicitor,
Marriage settlements short and explicit are:
  The only condition appearing
    On the part of the Fairy, was this:
      That her bridegroom should never say
      Save under his breath,
  Or out of her hearing.
A clause which no hubby could well take an
  And their life was so happy and gay,
  What a pity one terrible day,
  When preparing to go to a tournay,
    That a rash word should spoil it!
All was ready some time for their journe
And the fairy's white palfrey
Was wild to be stall-free,
  But the fairy was still at her toilet.
And her husband was getting
The fidgets, and fretting,
And swore they'd be late,
Had a mind not to wait,
And was wrought to a highly excitab'

When the Peri came down in her brilliants and beauty,
  Dress'd quite to her mind,
    From her cap to her shoe-tie ;
    Or as the sweet elf
    Murmur'd half to herself,
  " Before, very well ! really not bad behind !"
Quoth the lord of Argouges,
  What with feathers and rouge,
  Cap, mantle, and shoes,
  (Nota Bene—She never had seen
  Steel-petticoats, or crinoline.)
  You take, my fair lady,
  So long to get ready,
  Are such a slow coach, (how this slang must have
      shock'd her !)
  I'd far rather send you for Death, than a doctor !
    Oh, dear, let us all, old and young,
    Reflect that a word
  Tho' vain and absurd,
May stretch hearts on the rack,
Can be never call'd back,
  And watch well the lips and the Tongue !
At that sad monosyllable
  The Fairy hath melted in air !
  And the Lord of Argouges in despair,
  His life any longer to bear,
'Pon honor is ill able !
  And every night, a figure in white
Flits the castle around,
Or floats o'er the mound,
  And the servants all holding their breath,
And hiding their heads
Far down in their beds,
  Hear a voice cry, Death, Death !
And long very much for day light.

MORAL FOR GENTLEMEN.

Let each husband beware
How he ever says, Death, to his wife!
  But take most particular care,
If he scold (which between me and you,
He never should do),
  To call her, my Life!

MORAL FOR LADIES.

If Ladies, in dressing, the time only reckon'd,
The first dressing would not be cause of a second.

EPIGRAM.

Says Jove to Cupid, come my little man,
  Give up that Bow—no more of this abuse!
Quoth Cupid, Governor, you've been a Swan;
  Don't be a Goose!

SONNET.

FROM THE ITALIAN OF FAUSTINA MARATTA ZAPPI.

Where now mine own Sweet Son, where are they now,
  The eyes' bright glance, and front from sorrow sure?
  The lips' light play, with ever-changing lure,
And the smooth arching of the graceful brow.
Alas, beneath the fever fell they bow,
  That riots in thy blood, past hope or cure,
  And pours its venom through those veins so pure,
And answers with Death, Death! a mother's vow.

For oh, too well I see how brief a space
　My child will stay with me, and fate severe
Accuse in vain; run is my darling's race!
　Yet sorrow's fount is frozen so by fear,
That oft I bend above thy pallid face,
　And cannot bathe its beauty with a tear.

DREAM OF THE PAST.

At Danish post a passing guest,
I stopp'd to give my horses rest,
When light stept in a maiden young
　'Twixt girl and woman, say fifteen;
I spoke to her in German tongue,
　'Twas Dutch to both, I ween;
And ask'd how many lovers yet
She counted? ah, the young coquette,
She laugh'd outright, then look'd aside,
A blush that would have grac'd a bride
Flew o'er her cheek the while she cried,
　　　　　Ich weiss nicht was ist Liebe!

Methought could I but stay with thee,
Or Time alas delay with me,
And were this brain not full of care,
　This weary heart chill'd to its core,
How blest dear girl thy lot to share,
　And teach thee such sweet lore!
But I must hurry hurry on,
To be forgotten soon as gone,
While Norman lovers round thee throng,
　With words I wot not, on each tongue;
Awhile the burden of thy song
　　　　　Ich weiss nicht was ist Liebe!

I fill'd a glass of horrid stuff,
Some Cherry-poison, but enough,
It serv'd to pledge the maiden's health.
    I slipp'd a ring within her glove,
A simple one—no sign of wealth;
    And told her soon to love;
To love but one, with one to mate,
Though grief, or joy should be her fate.
From all, to choose her one alone;
She thank'd me, and I thought her tone,
With words the same, more wistful grown,
            Ich weiss nicht was ist Liebe!

Long years have pass'd—it sometimes seems
That only in the land of dreams
I look'd upon that pretty Dane;
Yet there I've seen her since again,
And wonder'd had she learn'd to prove
The height of joy, the depth of pain,
The meaning of—I love.
And waking, hop'd that she hath now
A stalwart mate of open brow,
And children with their father's hair,
And mother's eyes; and trust that pair
Can look, more certainly than swear;
            Wir wissen was ist Liebe!

CONCETTO.

My Love and I look'd in each others eyes,
And started back with mutual surprise;
She, overjoyed to see a face so fair;
And I, dismay'd to view a spectre there!

"LYDIA, DIC, PER OMNES."

FREE TRANSLATION OF HORACE, LIB. I., ODE VIII.

Arrah why Lydia Dick, by the Powers above,
Will you ruin Jem Connor, and all for your love?
He that cared not a curse for the dust or the sun,
Ev'n on Donnybrook-road, 's now afraid of a run;
And never goes out with the Garrison hounds,
Or bitts his Welsh poney for two or three rounds.
As for olives, cigars, or a swim in the Liffey,
He'd eat Salamanders as soon in a jiffey.
At quoits and at cricket he pitched in, and threw,
And bowl'd and long-stopp'd, until all black and blue:
Now he'd sculk, were we order'd to leather the French,
Like the son of Miss Thetis, the fishified wench:
I believe in my soul he'd sell out, or knock under,
Had the regiment a chance even Paris to plunder.
Late a brick, now a spoon, he was hearty, is sick;
Ah then maybe you'd let him alone, Lyddy Dick?

"TEUCER SALAMINA, PATREMQUE."

LIB. I. END OF ODE VII.

When Teucer his father and Salamis fled,
  Not fretting before he departed,
But winding a light poplar wreath round his head,
While his temples dropt wine, he thus manfully said
  To his mess-mates, all dumb, and downhearted.

Wherever our fortune, more kind than a father,
  May pilot us Lads, let us fare!
With Teucer as Skipper, around him come gather (
With Teucer for Soothsayer, who but will rather
  Trust him that we've nought to despair?

Brave boys, who have weather'd worse gales by my side,
A new Salamis soon shall cast doubts o'er the pride
    Of the old—so Apollo discovers:
Now chase care with wine-cups, whatever betide,
    On the Big Plain, to-morrow, the Rovers!

SACRIFICE TO THE GRACES.

Wit and learning are all very well in their place;
But how can they ever be so, without Grace?

There liv'd a philosopher once in old Greece,
    His nomen was Anaximander,
He had brains for half Athens—men there were no
    geese—
    But about as much grace as a gander.

After all, these philosopher chaps are but men,
    And his heart was both loving and tender,
He sigh'd at the Ladies; they laugh'd at him then,
    And for fools scorn'd poor Anaximander.

Then he hied to a Friend, and he show'd his discerning,
    When to Him he cried, Hard is my fate, oh!
The pet of the petticoats 'spite of his learning,
    A real good fellow was Plato!

Oh, teach me to please! To gain sooner my end,
    Let my life, quoth he, follow *your* traces!
Plato smil'd; Since the women reject them, my friend,
    Go, offer your vows to the Graces!

A word to the wise—to their temple he went,
 The Trio their smiles scarce concealing,
Before the wreath'd Beauties so oddly he bent,
 To see such a Novice at kneeling.

But they are the kindest of heav'nly .pow'rs,
 To philosophers just as to shepherds,
They sent back their Votary crown'd with rich flow'rs,
 And the ladies no longer were—leopards.

At Athens he grew quite the rage in a trice,
 And when he found similar cases,
He said, My good Pedant, take Plato's advice,
 And sacrifice more—to the Graces!

EASTERN APOLOGUE.

Thus spoke a Pasha to his prudent Vizier,
And brave Captain-general; Ministers! Hear!
It is hopeless much coin to amass I'm afraid,
And to keep a large army; a choice must be made.
Sire, said the Vizier, if you stick to the money,
You'll soon have the men; set a Bowl here of Honey,
If you fancy your servant speaks folly, or lies:
So said, and so done—when some myriads of flies
Came thronging, and clinging, and buzzing the while;
Lo! said the Vizier, and salaam'd with a smile.
Then the General spoke, No mistake, it's all right,
But I pray you just make the same trial, by Night;
If the flies should repair to the Honey-bowl then,
Degrade me at once, and disband all my men.
Night came; it was done—not a fly could be found,
And the gallant old General still held his ground.

REFLECTION.

Stint your Army and Navy in peace, and fine weather,
In War's stormy night can you bring them together?

IDEA FROM ST. FRANCIS DE SALES.

To mariners, afar who sail,
　Will Araby be known
By rich aroma on the gale,
　From that blest region blown.

Thus, of a far more happy land,
　Presentiments are giv'n,
To him, who at the prow doth stand,
　Aspiring after Heav'n.

THE EPICURE.

IMITATION OF COWPER.

I knew a Poet once, a meagre wight,
By day with hunger pinch'd, with cold at night;
I ask'd him to my meal, prepared my best,
And smil'd to see him eat it with such zest;
And laud the fish, flesh, fowl, and quaff the wine
From Woody Island, that had cross'd the Line;
From Xeres skin, or fam'd Oporto's vine.
But when my Bard had din'd, I smil'd still more,
To find him carp at all he prais'd before.
The Bread was not the same he lik'd to eat
Bought at the one good baker's, Grafton-street—
Nor was the Water near so pure he thought,
As what himself a mile or more oft brought,
From limestone Spring—my pump—a horrid doubt—
Was't iron? Yes! The murder then was out;
And the Potatoes, they were very fine,
Yet not so good as where he oft could dine

For sixpence; thus my gentleman found fault
With the whole meal, (except, I think, the Salt),
And own'd his preference for one plain dish,
And not to stuff fruit, pastry, fowl, and fish.
Reader thou now hast learn'd what I was taught,
And thy experience is more cheaply bought,
That no man is too humble or too poor,
To play the most fastidious Epicure.

EVEN SONG.

FROM CLAUDIUS' GERMAN, MODERNIZED.

"This Song" (we should rather call it a Hymn), "is not put here
to swell the number, but to give a hint of what the best popular
Songs (things that are and will be), should contain. The Song-
book is the people's Bible, their consoler, and their best recrea-
tion."—HERDER.

The moon is upward steering,
The golden stars appearing,
  In heav'n so bright and clear;
Dark lowers the forest-shadow,
While rising from the meadow,
  The white mist stalks, a shape of fear!

The earth looks still and pale,
Behind her twilight veil,
  Pensive, yet very fair,
A chamber cool and quiet,
Where day's distress and riot,
  Sleep and forgetfulness repair.

Look on the round moon yonder,
So beautiful, but ponder
   That one half she doth hide,
Like many things far nigh'r,
That wake a warm desire,
   Because we only see one side.

Poor mortals, vain and idle !
And yet how hard to bridle
   Our pride, and own the soul,
Maugre our wind-spun wisdom,
Each science, art, and system,
   Still wand'ring farther from the goal.

God, may our thoughts be holy !
Not fix'd on short-liv'd folly,
   Nor fed on shows of sense ;
Oh, may they bow before Thee,
And child-like, still adore Thee,
   In simple loving Confidence !

ON NEGLECTING TO RETURN A LADY'S SALUTE.

A chariot pass'd, from which a lovely face,
   While flitting by, vouchsaf'd a smile and bow;
Wond'ring I gazed, nor had the timely grace
   To doff the berrad from my puzzled brow.

Yet, lady, thou wilt only smile the more,
   Unconscious slight is easily forgiv'n ;
A face like thine I might have seen before,
   But fancied it was in a dream of heav'n.

And ev'n though spirits, stooping to this earth,
  Might deign to own a flow'r from Adam's stem,
Thy servant was a weed too little worth,
  Dear lady, to be recognis'd by them.

Another reason why I was misled,
  And which alone would save me from reproaches,
In all of angels I had ever read,
  There was no record that they kept their coaches.

FROM THE SPANISH, IN PART.

Men christen me the Love-defying;
And I am dying!
  As woman's lip may ne'er betray
    Her smouldering and wasting heart,
    What recks the world of hidden smart?
  Too cold, too gay, to feel, they say,
Her loveknots are of fashion's tying;
And I am dying!

I laugh and jest in lieu of sighing,
And I am dying!
  Love is consuming me in youth,
    As sure, though not so fast a fire
    As wraps a Hindoo widow's pyre;
  But if, like her, I smile, forsooth,
They fancy me on roses lying;
And I am dying!

LE GRENIER.

BERANGER.

I revisit the spot where my youth went to school,
  Dame Poverty's lessons compell'd to attend.
I was twenty; my sweetheart was such a young fool;
  And I somehow ne'er wanted a song or a friend.
I laugh'd at the world with its follies and glories,
  My spring had no fear of cold winter to mar it;
How merrily then did I dash up six stories—
  At twenty, how grandly one lives in a garret!

It was but a garret, there can't be a doubt,
  For there stood my bed, so uneasy and small,
Here my little deal table; and now I make out
  Three lines of a coal-written verse on the wall.
Oh, pleasures of youth which we barely can snatch,
  Ere time, the old curmudgeon, grumbles, I bar it,
For you, to my uncle, how oft went my watch—
  At twenty, one don't count the hours in a garret.

Ah, Ninon, my treasure, again rattle in, do!
  So pretty and gay, with a bonnet bran new,
And hang your shawl gracefully over the window,
  For why need our opposite neighbours peep through?
That pure muslin-dress, 'twere a pity to spoil it,
  Such nice inner curtains 'twill make when we're
    married,
I never ask'd then who had paid for your toilet;
  At twenty how blindly one loves in a garret.

With my friends one great day a Lucullus was I;
  How I got them heav'n knows, but I spent twenty
    francs,
When a shout reach'd our salon adjoining the sky,
  Napoleon, Marengo, the gallant French ranks.

Bom, bom, roar'd the cannon, we cheer'd and we sung,
   And quaff'd—I have never since tasted such claret!
Kings shall ne'er conquer France! we all cried;—we
     were young;
   At twenty how gaily one drinks in a garret!

But away from a spot with sweet memories rife!
   Far hence are those days, so regretted, so dear:
I would willingly give all the rest of my life
   For but one of the months that heav'n granted me
     here.
To dream of love, pleasure, or folly, or fame,
   To dissipate life ere regret may debar it,
With Hope in the distance still shining the same,
   At twenty, oh, what a grand place is a garret!

TO ——

JUVENILE VERSES.

I.

Another day with time hath done!
I watch the flushed and weary Sun,
With envy that his course is run.

II.

Prophetic be the glance he gave,
Ere calmly sinking 'neath the wave;
It augur'd of a quiet grave.

III.

For life's spring-tide is ebbing fast,
Its fever dream is well nigh past,
And one may hope for rest at last.

IV.

And then for me no sullen knell
Startle the laughing throng, to tell,
A soul has bidden earth farewell.

V.

No hired mourner, car of gloom,
With sable, or with snowy plume,
To mock a marriage with the tomb.

VI.

No coffin-plate, no churchyard stone;
Unknown in life, in death unknown,
I do but ask to lie alone.

VII.

Where trees an arching shade may spread,
And wild-flowers creep about my bed,
And blithe birds carol over head.

VIII.

And frolic little children play,
As innocent and blithe as they,
And ev'rything keep holiday!

IX.

Ev'n Thou perchance in summer-heat,
Will find that sod a welcome seat,
Nor dream what moulders at thy feet!

THE SERENADE, FROM UHLAND.

What strange sweet sounds awaken me,
  As with a gentle kiss?
Oh mother, see; who can it be,
  So late an hour as this?

Nothing I see, love; nought I hear,
  Sleep on, of pain beguil'd,
No serenade now woos thine ear
  Thou darling, suffering child!

Not earthly music may it be
  That makes me feel so light!
The songs of angels summon me;
  Oh, mother dear, good night!

N A PAINTING OF FEDERICO AMERLING

*Representing a young girl gazing on a Miniature, and a boy playing
beside her.*

FROM THE ITALIAN.

Not sleep, nor yet a wakeful ken
  Within those fring'd orbits lies;
What earthly thought may image then
  Her heav'nly-pensive eyes?

The vesper hour of semi-light,
  When pearl and purple, dark and pale
Commingle so, it is not night,
  Though day begins to fail.

A sweet illusion can command
  Life for that face to us unknown,
Rapt on whose traits, to spirit-land
  The loving girl hath flown.

Oh, precious ecstacy of thought,
  By which an hour, while flitting fast
From that profound abyss is caught,
  And dreamt of, ere 'tis past.

She sees a face we cannot see,
  A coming change we cannot tell;
A bridal-room, where wont to be
  A virgin couch and cell.

The images her fancy moulds,
  Are pure as light of summer skies,
That through the crimson curtain-folds
  Assumes their rosy dyes.

Oh, hush, dear boy, from that fair scene
  Disturb her not; too soon in sooth
The shadows on that filmy screen
  Must yield to sober truth!

Not yet to life let her awaken,
  Its sighs repress'd, and secret tears;
The heart-despair to be forsaken,
  The absence of long years.

The glow-worm only in the shade
  Displays her tiny lamp, withdrawn
From busy day, and, ah, to fade
  With the first peep of dawn.

And thus, my boy, by word or wile
  Of thine the charmed chain were riven;
Oh, let her wander yet a while
  In her fantastic heav'n!

Angelic shapes, no dumb dead hues,
  No work of pictur'd art are ye!
Could art our senses so confuse
  With nature's mastery?

Whatever love hath cull'd most sweet,
　With melancholy's softest sighs,
Whate'er of grief, or joy, repeat
　The tend'rest memories.

The incense of the air in spring,
　The chasten'd thoughts that oft excite
In bards who court dusk evening
　The closing wings of night.

Ephemeral hopes of life's short May,
　Like dew-drops on some aged thorn;
Pale moon-beams, the bright sunny ray,
　And buds that earth adorn.

All, all have shed their influence,
　Ye wonder-works of shape and hue,
Upon his spirit and his sense
　Whose pencil painted you!

———

FROM OLIVER BASSELIN.

There's a war in which for valor I am like Leonidas,
'Tis where we strive with mighty bowl, and many a
　　brimming glass,
For a round of good grape-liquor better suits my heart
　　and head,
Than your rounds of cruel grape-shot that so soon leave
　　people dead.

The shot I love is when the corks jump out of cider
　　bottles,
And the barrels which I relish are all charg'd up to
　　their throttles;

For jolly tuns are my great guns, which batter without
 fail,
At thirst—the sole Sebastopol I ever would assail.

It is a very brutal thing, at least as I opine,
If people's heads are splitting, that 'tis not with mighty
 wine,
Instead of cuts with sabres, for now what's the use of
 fame,
If you are dead, and cannot hear when any shout your
 name?

If you drink a trifle overmuch, why either you escape,
 or
You feel a little headachy, and in a kind of vapour;
But then you go to sleep, and awaken free from pain,
But lose your head in honor's bed, and you never wake
 again.

'Tis better then to hide your nose within a fragile glass,
And safer than a helmet far, whatever comes to pass,
So instead of drum or trumpet, a mute guide I follow
 quicker,
The ivy-bush that beckons me where I get the best of
 liquor.

And better by a blazing fire to quaff the muscadel,
Than pace the rampart up and down, a weary Sentinel,
To follow lead I'm seldom known in taverns at default,
But I'd hate to follow leaders to a breach, or an assault.

However I must fairly own I never lov'd excess,
No drunkard base like many a one who talks of drink
 far less,
But good wine, that makes us sorrow-free, with friends
 and song so gay,
The promise I have vow'd to thee, religiously I'll pay.

THE RETURN OF THE DEAD.

OLD DANISH—FROM GERMAN OF OEHLENSCHLAEGER.

To the castle Sir Sweno spurs away,
For a maiden fair he weds to-day.

They liv'd together for sev'n years' space,
Each opened on a baby's face.

Then death's dark wing the land o'ershaded,
And the sweet mother-rose, it faded.

To the tow'r Sir Sweno rides away,
For he will wed with another May.

Again a bride home with him came,
I trow a wicked and haughty dame.

And as she through the court did fare,
The little ones all stood weeping there.

The children sev'n ill did she greet;
She spurn'd them from her with her feet.

She gave those bairns nor beer nor bread
Ye shall learn what hunger means, she said.

She took their coverlets soft and blue,
Said, Musty straw is too good for you.

Of the large wax-lights she left no spark,
Ye may learn methinks to lie in the dark.

The children sobb'd till night full sore,
And their mother heard, and could sleep no more.

The woman heard in her coffin small,
Oh I must go to my children all.

Before God's face she bow'd down low,
And may I not to the children go?

So long she stay'd, so strong she pray'd,
He let her loose to the childrens' aid.

And may'st stay there until cock-crow,
Then to thy grave again shalt go.

There shot a might through mould'ring bones,
That burst thick walls and marble stones,

And as she flash'd the village through,
Long howl'd the hound his wild halloo.

And when she pass'd the castle door,
Her eldest daughter she stood before.

Why art thou standing here my child,
And where are thy sisters meek and mild?

You look a lady fair and fine,
But mother you may not be of mine.

I cannot be fine or fair, I trow,
I was laid in a coffin too long ago.

Mother was fair, but her cheeks were red,
And yours are as wan, as you were dead!

And when they entered the gloomy hall,
There sobbing stood the bairnies all.

She cherish'd the first, the second she smooth'd,
She kiss'd the third, and the rest she sooth'd.

She lifted on her lap the least,
And gave it from her breast a feast.

She said to her eldest daughter, Dear,
Go bid Sir Sweno hasten here.

And from his chamber when he came,
Her words were fire, her eyes were flame.

I left behind me bread and beer,
My children pine in hunger here.

I left blue coverlets warm and fine,
My children are bedded in straw, like swine.

I brought you many a huge wax light,
My children are wailing in fear and night.

I tell you this; if I come again,
'T will be all over with you then !

The second wife call'd from bed to the first,
Good troth your bairns shall be well nurs'd !

The hound scarce yelp'd, or a footstep pass'd,
But the children got their broth full fast.

Whenever they heard the dog's low howl,
She fear'd the Dead at the door might prowl.

Yea, whether the wind would whistle, or roar,
They fear'd the Dead Mother would come once more.

VERSES TO MY FIRST-BORN.

From the French—pretended author, Clotilde de Surville, born
about 1405—real author, Joseph Etienne de Surville, born 1755!
(or Charles Vanderbourg, the Editor, who published this, and
other poems in a pretended old dialect, Paris, 1804). If Joseph
Etienne was not a male Mrs. Harris, he at least created plenty
of Ladies like her; viz., a whole school of Poetesses, with sam-
ples of their poems, and anecdotes of their lives, all being purely
imaginary—as perhaps he was himself—for Mr. Charles Van-
derbourg (if there was even such a person) the so-called Editor,
is probably the author of the whole Fiction. Be that as it may,
these verses, and several of the others, are extremely pretty and
plausible.

Oh Baby dear, thy Father's miniature,
   Sleep on the bosom which thy lips have prest;
No longer may those little lids endure
   The weight of slumber; close them then in rest.

My Baby-boy, whose eyes so soft and tender,
   Enjoy repose—no longer made for mine,
I watch for thee, thy nurse, and thy defender,
   And prize a Life that watches over thine.

Sleep on, my constant care, my beauteous pet,
   Upon this bosom, as within, erewhile;
Thy childish babble may not bless me yet,
   But oft I read the language of thy smile.

Perhaps when presently awaking, thou
   Wilt smile at me, with ever new surprise;
And yet I think thou seem'st to know me now,
   And lov'st to see thine image in my eyes.

His tiny fingers have released the cup,
   The mother fount which he had quaff'd at will;
Ah, had he pow'r to drink that bosom up,
   The longing of his thirst would feed it still!

Sweet infant son, whom almost I adore,
  My business now in life, and only play,
Still gazing on thee, I would gaze the more,
  And deem too short to see thee, night and day.

Out-stretch'd his chubby arms on slumber's bosom,
  He stirs not, hears not; scarce I feel his breath,
And but for these faint hues of apple-blossom,
  My boy might seem within the clasp of death.

Stay, stay, lov'd child! I shudder with affright;
  Look up, and chase so horrible a thought!
Dear babe, a moment look upon the light,
  Though my repose with loss of thine be bought.

Oh fool, he sleeps; relieved, I breathe again;
  Light dreamlets fan him with a fairy wing;
When shall I have One far away, ah when!
  Beside me to enjoy his wakening?

When he, by whom thy hold on life was giv'n,
  My youthful spouse fair as the cherubim,
Will see thee—oh presentiment of heav'n!
  Hold out thy pure and tiny hands to him;

How will he doat upon thy first caress,
  Challenge each kiss, and claim thy ev'ry touch,
But think not to exhaust his tenderness;
  For his Clotilda he will save as much.

Methinks in thee he views his image now,
  The large eyes, bluish grey, that flash yet melt;
The turn of cheek so graceful, and the brow
  So grand, that Cupid rather jealous felt;

But I shall ne'er feel jealous of his life
  With thee divided, nor imagine wrong,
When thou like him, wilt make a happy wife;
  Ah, leave her not to linger quite so long!

My words thou dost not hear; oh, folly-fraught,
  If quite awake, how could he comprehend?
Poor little Infant! of its threads of thought,
  We do not hold one disentangled end.

Sad reason comes too soon; too soon will cease
  This interval, as with us all, with thee!
Remain then, babe, in thine unconscious peace,
  And would thou might'st preserve its memory!

ON THE MARGIN.

His eyes soft fire, his roses' very tint,
  His air, his features, all I love on earth!
But why surprised? did he not all imprint?
  From me what fainter copy could have birth?

GUDRUN'S GRIEF.

FROM THE ANGLO-SAXON.

It was the hour when Gudrun
  Loath'd life, and long'd to die;
And ruefully was sitting
  Her Sigurth's body bye.
And sigh'd not, wept not, neither
Clapp'd both her hands together;
  Nor mourn'd like other women,
  For husband lost, or leman.

Came Earls then to upbraid her,
  The sagest and the chief,
And fain they would dissuade her,
  From the hardness of her grief :
But Gudrun's eyes were burning,
She could not weep, though yearning
  For tears, her heart did languish,
  And well nigh burst with anguish.

Then of Counties erst so bold
  Came widow'd wives, each one
Bedeck'd in ruddy Gold,
And with Gudrun sate them down ;
  And each her grief told over,
  For husband, child, or lover,
  Till their own eyes 'gan to glitter,
  With those memories full bitter.

And some had borne yet more,
  In slav'ry dark and deep,
She heard their trials sore,
  But not yet could Gudrun weep
Tho' for her warrior mourning,
Her heart to stone was turning ;
As rigid, mute, and moody,
She sate beside his body.

To the elder women then,
  Quoth Gulrond, Guika's daughter,
"Doth not each matron ken,
  Or Time hath little taught her,
That for young widows' solace,
The wisest words are follies ?"
Forsooth it was her study,
To hide no more the Body.

The pall away she sweeps
　From Sigurth where he lies;
Heaves the head up, till it sleeps
　Upon Gudrun's lap, and cries,
Look down upon thy love now,
As tho' he breath'd above now,
Lay mouth on his cold lips, too,
Clasp him in death's eclipse, too.

And Gudrun's frozen eye
　Fell low a moment there;
She saw the gory dye
　That streak'd her hero's hair:
She saw the orbs late glowing,
All dull and leaden showing,
And his bosom's fortress gor'd,
And the spot where ran the sword.

Her face then Gudrun bow'd,
　And in the cushions hid,
She made no yammer loud,
　But the tears gush'd out unbid,
Dishevelled lay her head then,
Her cheek relax'd, grew red then,
And the heart's rain, set free,
Ran downward to her knee.

BONAPARTE.

FROM DE LAMARTINE.

On a lone rock where waves incessant wail,
As tho' some foam-flake wafted by the gale,
　The seaman eyes a Tomb, yon Island's token;
Its narrow stone time hath not yet embrown'd,
And 'mid green rush and ivy, wreathing round,
　Behold, a Sceptre broken!

Here lies ; no name ?   Demand of earth that name !
Stamp'd wide in characters of blood and flame,
　　From Tanais' shore to Kedar's heights afar,
On marble, bronze, the breast of many a brave,
Aye, and the heart of every regal slave
　　That crouch'd beneath his car !

Since the great Twain, from age to age by Fame
Resounded, ne'er hath flown a mortal name
　　So far on wings of wonder and of fear ;
The foot of man, by ev'ry breath effaced,
A deeper print on earth had never traced,
　　And its last step was, Here !

A child's three paces length, here is he laid,
And not a murmur from the mighty shade,
　　Ev'n tho' a foeman's foot be passing o'er ;
Unheard the gnat hums round that thunder-brow,
The wave unheard, tho' dashing still, as now,
　　Against the rocky shore.

Shade of the fallen Monarch, fear from me
No insult to thy voiceless majesty !
　　The Lyre hath never outrag'd tombs ; in sooth
Glory's asylum ever was the Grave,
Nought should pursue a mem'ry thither, save
　　Inevitable Truth.

Curtain'd by cloud thy cradle and thy tomb,
The levin-bolt, that seams the tempest-gloom,
　　Slaying ere seen ; in war so swift, and strong ;
In peace like Nile, whom Memphis half adores,
While nameless yet its wavelets wash the shores
　　Of Memnon, silent long.

P

Heaven's thrones seem'd vacant, Earth's without their
    kings,
When Victory bore thee up on rapid wings,
   Over each modern Brutus, to a Crown.
The age whose foamy torrent downward bore
Customs, Kings, Gods, itself recoil'd before
   A new Achilles' frown.

Error begirt with myriads, thou'st defied,
And like fierce Jacob, struggling in thy pride,
   Its phantoms sank beneath a mortal's weight;
Profaning names deem'd sacred, or sublime,
Like reckless hand of sacrilegious crime
   Poising the altar's freight.

Thus when an age grown impotent, out-worn,
By its own hands in vain delirium torn,
   Raves in its chains, and bellows, I am free;
Some hero from the dust at once supreme,
Rises, and strikes; it wakens, and its dream
   Yields to reality.

Ah, hadst thou bas'd the Throne on ancient right,
Nor stain'd with blood religion's robe of white,
   Warrior-avenger were thy title now;
Pope, king, avenging, greater far than they,
With what sweet incense, with how pure a ray,
   Had glory grac'd thy brow!

Fame, honour, freedom; all man's word-gods fell
Upon thine ear like some far booming bell,
   Monotonous and meaningless were all;
The only voices in thy breast that rang
And woke an echo, were the sabre-clang,
   The clarion's battle call.

Proud of disdaining what earth deifies,
Thou yet would'st sway her sceptre, and despise ;
 Thy march begin, each obstacle a foe,
Send forth thy will, too often Death's own dart ;
What tho' its course lay through a friendly heart,
 On sped the fated blow.

And ne'er to cheer the gloom of royalty,
The festive cup its nectar pour'd for thee,
 Another purple sparkled in thine eye ;
While still on guard, a sentinel in arms,
Thou could'st see beauty's smiling, tearful, charms,
 Without a smile or sigh.

Thy loves the clashing steel, the battle shout,
The dawn upon bright bayonets breaking out,
 Thy horse alone own'd thy caressing hand :
When with surging white, his billowy mane,
Like visible breeze sweeping some gory plain,
 He spurn'd the corse-strewn sand.

Filling unmov'd, or falling from a throne,
Beneath thy bosom seem'd a heart of stone,
 No love, no hate ; thy soul for thought was cast ;
An eagle in thy solitary sky,
To measure earth thou had'st the king-bird's eye,
 His claws to clutch her fast.

To gain the car of victory with a spring,
Trampling alike on tribune, and on king,
 With dazzling glories ev'n the wise to blind :
To forge a yoke temper'd as if by Fate,
And make a nation tremble 'neath its weight,
 Which law had fail'd to bind.

To be an age's theme ; its soul and life,
To silence envy, blunt ev'n freedom's knife,
  The tott'ring Earth to settle or to shake ;
Amid the death-flash by thine engines hurl'd,
To game against the gods, thy stake a world—
  From what a dream to wake !

Of what a downfal to survive the shock !
Flung by the whirlwind on a barren rock,
  Thy mantle dropt no mortal may assume ;
Fortune, thy goddess, in thy pride of place,
As a last favor left this little space,
  Between thy throne and tomb.

Oh, could I but have sounded that dark deep,
When memory of the past would silent sweep,
  Clad, like Remorse, athwart thy troubled soul !
When with arms folded on thiue ample chest,
O'er thy bent brow, with heavy thought opprest,
  The horror-cloud would roll !

The shepherd, standing on the river shore,
Observes his shadow lengthen more and more,
  As floating on the mirror-stream it plays ;
And standing thus, on greatness' barren height,
Thy shadowy self in memory's setting light
  Flitted o'er bygone days.

They roll'd before thee undular, sublime,
Emitting vivid gleams from time to time,
  With sound subdued like some far battle-song ;
A ray of glory oft thy visage caught,
Reflected from some fresher wave of thought
  Where thine eye linger'd long.

Death here upon a tott'ring bridge defying
While there the desert's sacred dust is flying,
  Now Jordan's wave thy shudd'ring steed doth part;
Yonder thy foot hath crumbled mountains down,
At home thy sword, unmated, turned a crown,
  But what a fearful start!

Why, conscience-stricken, thus avert thy view?
Why deeper pallor on that pallid hue?
  What spectres of the past thy soul appal?
A hundred villages in ruins smoking,
A score of battle-plains man's life-blood soaking?
  Glory hath cover'd all.

Can glory cover murder?   Stern remorse
His finger pointeth to a hero's corse,
  That pure young blood hath blighted all thy fame:
The wave that bore it, passing, never passed,
But ling'ring still, a vengeful murmur cast,
  Coupled with Condé's name.

As tho' a stain like that could e'er be lost,
His brow in vain with hurried hand he cross'd,
  The blood-spot only fresher blush'd, each time;
And as a seal, stamp'd by the hand supreme,
For ever there a burning diadem,
  It crown'd him with his crime.

Tyrant! this crime may make men ponder long,
If genius ever stoop'd so low to wrong,
  This stain will track thy chariot wheels throughout,
Thy name be flung in wild opinion's rage,
Cæsar, or Marius, from age to age,
  The sport of endless doubt.

Yet hast thou died as common mortals die,
As ere paid off the mower shuts his eye,
　　And sinks beside his scythe, with labour spent;
Leaning in silence on thy bloody sword,
Thou'st gone to gain requital from thy Lord,
　　Who knows his instrument.

'Tis said in pangs tho' tedious, seldom shown,
When left before eternity alone,
　　His eye uprais'd his Maker seem'd to seek;
The sign redeeming touch'd that gloomy brow,
And on his lip a name is trembling now,
　　He dareth not to speak.

Speak! it is He who made thee reign, who reigneth;
Who punisheth, yet suff'ring long, refraineth;
　　For us and heros different scales obtain :
He reads thy spirit; speak! to Him alone,
The slave and tyrant must alike atone,
　　For sceptre and for chain !

Clos'd is his coffin : God hath judg'd him : peace !
T' adjust his crimes with his achievements, cease;
　　Man's puny hand holds not such balance even;
Oh, who can sound the mercies of our God!
The genius of the chief he makes his rod,
　　May be his hold on Heav'n.

_____

HYMN TO POLAND.

VERSIFIED FROM DE LA MENNAIS.

Sleep, my Poland, in peace, and gain strength in the
　　gloom,
On that couch which thy tyrant imagines a tomb.

Deserted, betray'd, when thy bright brow grew pale,
Aghast Europe shudder'd, as through her there went
Thy foeman's wild yell, which she heard with a thrill,
Such as that of hyenas at night, sharp and shrill,
Gives the cowering traveller, wak'd in his tent.

Like the armour-clad knights an old abbey around,
On their tombs, lay the giant-form stretch'd on the
    ground,
They strew'd it with dust, all beclotted with gore,
And said—It will waken no more!

But thy sons widely scatter'd, bore with them thy
    story;
Where, where is the land hath no gleam of thy glory?
They told how the yoke of the tyrant fell shiver'd,
And Poland arose, from her dungeon deliver'd,
By the angel of God, with a glaive bar'd for slaughter,
And the heart of the Russian is turning to water!

How thy princes, thy people, the greatest, the least,
The warrior, the woman, the boy, and the priest,
Aye, the children, for thee fought and bled, sank and
    slept;
The hearers their faces bow'd low, and they wept.

In vain were the seeds of such martyrdom sown!
Is thy harvest then, Slavery, Poland, alone?
Turn'd to thee the lorn looks of the exil'd and brave,
How long shall they see but a grass-cover'd grave?

The cowardly despot defiles thy remains;
He loads the brave hands of thy soldiers with chains,
Nay, thy womens', some balm for his fear to afford,
And Siberia gleans what was left from the sword.

While flung into mines they are lost to the world,
He stands in his pride o'er the prostrated walls
Of thy temples, all crumbling to powder, till hurl'd
O'er the blood-bedew'd altar, the last of them falls!

Hush! what is that sound through the dark forest
    heard,
The moan of the wind—but what shape do you see
O'er the plain swiftly glancing? same passenger-bird
That seeks where its weary wing rested may be.

Is that all, is that all? see you not a Cross hover
O'er that point in the east the sun loves first to greet?
While at ev'ning, the rapt ear can vaguely discover
The blending of voices, mysterious, but sweet.

Now look on her brow, where, unruffled, though pale,
Hope is brooding, and lo! a faint smile on her lips,
Slightly quivers beneath the bright visions that sail
Through her sleep; shall that hopeful smile suffer
    eclipse?

No! glancing from heaven, see Faith on her heart,
Hath laid a warm hand, its long chill to unbind;
With the other, futurity's veil flings apart,
And points to where Liberty towers behind!

Sleep, my Poland, in peace, yet to wake from the gloom
Of the cradle, which tyranny takes for a tomb!

————

FROM THE FRENCH OF VICTOR HUGO.

Let the children alone! They so love to be there!
But the bubbles I blow, and you fancy so fair

May burst at the breath of a boy?
Can you think that such voices, and footsteps, and plays,
Would frighten the Muses and banish the Fays?
  Come, children, crowd on in your joy!

Run round me, wherever ye will, laugh and sing;
While your eyes dart, with gladness, the sunshine of
    Spring,
  And your voices leave echoes behind,
Sole sounds from without, void of sorrow or sin,
They disturb not the spirit that broodeth within,
  But take parts in the tune of the mind.

They are no friends of mine who send children away,
Do they think my worn heart feels less cheerful, less gay,
  When such faces are flocking around?
Oh no! In my nightmares of blood and of flame,
If a child's ringing laugh, or its curly head came,
  They brought balm in the sight, and the sound.

Their joys and their gestures remain in the room
When they leave it, their mem'ry may shed a perfume,
  Round verses though humble as mine;
Then Ye, who perchance may have felt, as ye read,
Thank the Children alone for the fragrance they shed,
  Like the dew of the dawn, on each line.

Come, Children; each garden, and staircase, and door,
Is open to you; shake each ceiling and floor,
  Shake your own little fat sides with laughter;
And as ye rush humming and buzzing along,
Like a fresh swarm of bees, oh my soul, and my song,
  And my blessing shall hover close after.

Seek *some refuge afar from this Babel of mirth,*
Ye who will; some old bachelor's Eden on earth,

Whose silence no youngster e'er marr'd;
But for Heaven's sake pray there may ne'er be exil'd
One ray of the sun, or one smile of the child,
   From the sky or the home of a bard!

But the accents the Muse whispers low in the ear,
Which the spirit bends down all enraptur'd to hear,
   Their noise and their sport will destroy?
Well, what do I care for the flatt'ry of fame,
The mock immortality circling a name,
   So I feel once again like a Boy!

What's Fame? a poor pebble dropt down a deep well;
Did you hear its last echo? How faintly it fell!
   A moment or two—it is past—
A life full of indigence, envy, or spite,
Dark dreams in the day, and long watches at night,
   In your grave to be slander'd at last!

Oh no! Give me life, give me love, give me leisure,
My little ones round me, my freedom and pleasure,
   Though Glory should shrink with affright,
And startled with laughter, my well chosen-words,
Be lost in the hubbub, a flock of small birds,
   When school-boys have put them to flight.

Yet from children there's nothing worth loving will
   turn,
The East pours for them liquid gold from her urn,
   And paints her rich insects, and flow'rs;
So poesy smiling, selects for her art,
Bright hopes and fresh feelings which warm the young
   heart,
  And preserves them, to renovate ours!

FABLE.

THE ORIGIN OF "A RUM 'UN TO LOOK AT, BUT A GOOD 'UN TO GO."

Miss Cray-fish, wandering one day
Along the river-side,
Sly Reynard met upon the way,
Who, when the shape he spied
Of this odd creature, wriggling so,
That rather sideway seem'd to go,
He marvel'd much at what he saw,
And not content to see,
Tumbled her over with his paw,
To feel what it could be.
At which the little lobster fish
Getting a sort of dizziness,
Cried out—"My friend, I really wish
You'd go about your business;
And as I'm letting you alone,
Pass on, and let me mind my own!"
"Yours?" said the Fox, with gibe and sneer,
"What *is* your business, my dear?
A courier, likely, by your style
Of going; 'tis the pace
That kills, and yet for half a mile
I'd venture on a race!"
"Done!" said the Cray-fish; "for my part,
I never *bet* above a pony."
Don Reynard's stare was almost stony—
"But never fear, I'll give some start,
I think a length may be enough;
Take it—and wait till I say, off!"
The fox with laughter nearly died,
He snicker'd till he fairly cried,
And press'd a paw to either side.

"But ev'ry little helps," quoth he,
"Like the wren's tears to fill the sea."
Then turning round exclaim'd—"All right?"
Miss Cray-fish crept upon his tail,
And said, "to beat you I'll go bail;
Like a steam-carriage, the old mail;
One to stop; two, to stay;
Three, to make ready, and four—away!"
On flew the Fox as though the hounds
Were at his brush, adown the wind;
He reach'd the goal with long light bounds,
And turn'd to look behind:
Yet thought, what folly! by my honor,
I'll never more set eyes upon her;
When Miss Cray gently letting go,
Cried out—"Holloa, my friend, holloa!
What do you mean by craning so?
That was a rather spicy burst,
But still you see which horse is first."
The Fox turn'd short, and to his cost
Finding that somehow he had lost,
"Astonied stood, and blank;" all o'er
He view'd Miss Cray, behind, before,
Who bridled and sidled, with a smile all the while;
Glad that there were no more beholders,
He heav'd a sigh, and shrugg'd his shoulders,
And said with a grin, as he fork'd out the tin,
And wish'd her a very hot berth—below;
"You're a rum 'un to look at, but a good 'un to go!"

THE DEATH OF HACO.

FROM THE NORSE.

Sweeping o'er the battle-plain,
Lo, the Choosers of the slain

Sent from Odin, hither come,
  For the prince of Ynga's race,
Whom a warrior's death they doom,
  Ere with Gods a dwelling-place.
Gondula, on tall lance leaning,
Mutter'd thus their mystic meaning,
"Let the Gods enlarge their ring,
Haco's foes invite the king,
On his warriors too they call,
Soon to enter Odin's hall."
Fairer more than mortal, They,
  Shrouded under helm and shield,
On their steeds, the coming fray,
  Each seem'd scanning far a-field.
Haco heard in fierce disdain,
  "Why the battle thus dispose?
Are we worthy but to gain
  From the Gods such boons as those?"
"Who give conquest?" murmur'd she,
Chase thy foes? We, Haco, we!
Sisters speed!
Each urge her steed,
Over verdure-clad abodes,
Homes of ever-happy Gods,
Till to Odin's royal home,
Heralds of a King we come!
Odin heard, and swift he said,
Hermod, hail the mighty Dead!
Braga too, go forth to meet him,
Worthy he that Gods should greet him!
Haco enters from the fight,
  Dripping still with foemen's blood;
"Ha!" quoth he, at Odin's sight,
  "That's a grisly looking God!"
Braga answer'd, "Doubt no wrong,
Terror of the hostile throng!

Haste thy brethern eight to meet,
And assume thy god-like seat;
Friends in all these Heroes, hail;
Haste to quaff the foaming ale!"
Cried the valiant king, "Enough!
   Yet I keep my armour on;
Casque and cuirass when we doff,
   Danger cometh—they are gone;
Ever arm'd and on their guard,
Warriors keep watch and ward."
Then each hero from his throne
Hail'd king Haco; then was known
Who, while yet on earth, had giv'n
Off'rings worthiest of Heav'n.
Blest the day a king is born,
   God-belov'd, to do their will!
Mortals keep that happy morn,
   In their mem'ry hallow'd still;
Fenris, furious wolf, unbound,
First shall fly at foes around,
Ere so good a king have birth
On the weary widow'd earth.
   Riches perish, parents die,
   Fattest pastures ravag'd lie,
But king Haco hath a home
With the Gods—and years to come
   Must his people mourn and sigh!

MY COAT.

FROM BERANGER.

My good old coat, oh, give not o'er!
   Let us still be at one;
Ten years I've brush'd thee—say what more
   Could Socrates have done?

Should Fortune, in our thread-bare state,
　Wage warfare without end,
Oppose, like me, philosophy to fate;
　But do not let us part, my good old friend!

I well remember, though so long,
　The day I wore thee, new;
My birth-day, and my friends in song
　Paid us all honour due;
Now thine age honours me, at least
　Warm hands they still extend,
And each kind heart still bids us to the feast—
　Then do not let us part, my dear old friend!

A darn along the back I see,
　Sweet memory of old,
When feigning from my love to flee,
　I felt her tighten'd hold;
And thou gav'st way; that dreadful rent,
　How hard it prov'd to mend!
Two days Lisette on that great labour spent;
　Then do not let us part, my good old friend!

In atmospheres of musk or amber
　Have I e'er poison'd thee?
Or risk'd thee in some antichamber
　To scorn from a grandee?
When France for ribbands—worthy goal
　Of faction, could contend,
A simple field-flow'r grac'd thy button-hole;
　Then do not let us part, my dear old friend!

And fear no more the courses vain
　Our youth alike hath run,
Those days of pleasure dash'd with pain,
　Of mingled show'r and sun!

Soon, far away, whate'er the weather,
  Without thee must I wend,
Then wait a bit, and we will go together;
  Let us not part till then, my good old friend!

THE DEVIL'S DEATH.

BERANGER.

List a miracle veracious!
  Think not that my fancy paints,
Glorify great Saint Ignatius,
  Lord of all our little saints.
By a ruse—'twould be uncivil
  Of a saint if worse were said,
Listen how he kill'd the devil,;
  The devil's dead, the devil's dead!

Satan, catching him at dinner,
  Cried, hob-nob! old chum of mine!
Tope! quoth Ig., but tipp'd the sinner
  Holy water in his wine;
Satan, reckless of mishaps,
  Gulp'd it, grinn'd, and took to bed;
Cholera ensued—collapse—
  The devil's dead, the devil's dead!

Dead! Alas, cried ev'ry friar,
  Who will buy our holy lambs?
Dead! sang canons, octaves higher,
  Who will pay us for our psalms?
In dark conclave soon they gather,
  Gold was gone; their bosoms bled;
Orphans, ye have lost a father!
  The devil's dead, the devil's dead!

Love awaking, fear is flying;
  What rich gifts she wrung from men!
Bigotry's dull flame is dying;
  Who will light it up again?
If the world relief may hope
  From our yoke, the truth will spread,
God be greater than the Pope;
  The devil's dead, the devil's dead!

Cried Ignatius, cold and grim,
  Give his throne, ye ghostly elves!
No one cared a curse for him;
  I will frighten kings themselves.
War and murder, plague and thievings,
  Shall but feed the Order's Head;
Heav'n may shift upon our leavings,
  The devil's dead, the devil's dead!

All responded, bravo! Come,
  Let us crown thee in thy gall!
Then the Order, prop of Rome,
  Flung o'er heav'n a funeral-pall:
Sorrow on the angels fell;
  Let us mourn for Man! they said;
Lo! Ignatius, heir of hell!
  The devil's dead, the devil's dead!

TIME ABOUT.

When Kitty was a little maid,
  Just in her teens, and very pretty,
My cousin Mary was afraid
  That I would make a fool of Kitty.
But after half a dozen years,
  At ease may cousin Mary be,
Oh! not at all, for now she fears
  That Katherine makes a fool of me.

HANG SPRING!

BERANGER.

All winter I could see her sit
   At work beside her window there,
And ogles would between us flit,
   And kisses seem'd to cross in air;
Through yonder lindens, leafless then,
   We peep'd, and smil'd, and sigh'd—alack!
Their leaves are pushing out again;
   Accurséd spring is coming back!

And those sweet looks will soon be lost;
   How oft I watch'd her there below,
While she would feed, in winter-frost,
   The little birds that lov'd her so!
How they would chirp, and bill, and crow,
   And at her pretty fingers peck!
What a delightful thing is snow!
   Hang spring! it's always coming back.

For then I saw her ev'ry morn,
   When her light slumber fled away,
Fresh as Aurora, newly-born,
   Withdraw the curtain of the day;
For else, at night her course I'd keep,
   Her lamp the star to guide my track,
I'd watch with her, with her would sleep,
   Hang spring! it's always coming back.

Oh! winter, haste with snow and rain!
   Oh! would that I could hear ye still,
Gay hailstones, slapping at the pane,
   Or jumping off the window-sill!

Spring here? what's spring to me, its vile
    Fine days, and flow'rs, if I must lack
The hope to see her sunny smile?
    Damn spring! it's always coming back!

———

THE CHASE OF COOLAGHGORAN.

I'll chant you a stave of a desperate chase,
From its length and its strength; from the weather and
    pace;
Twenty-five Irish miles, and in less than two hours,
Is a meal for most horses and hounds, by the pow'rs!

At as near nine as eight Coolaghgoran we drew,
For a thief that in former runs Tony* well knew;
My brave spotted fox, the Light Infantry† true,
Early fed, and well match'd, will soon open on you!

How cheering to mark, from the soft-rising ground,
The fox-hunters gather as morn broke around!
You would fancy some loadstone kept drawing them
    still;
'Twas the pack in its pride on the brow of the hill!

The taking his drag was a train set alight,
It is touch'd, and where are they? See there—out of
    sight!
While Madman proclaims the good news at first dash,
And the rest all cry ditto! and off with a crash!

---

    * Tony, the huntsman.   † Name of pack.

But while skirting a covert, within the first mile,
A fresh fox! and we split—death and fury! awhile
Our fears and exertions no rest had—no bounds,
Till the line was maintain'd by five couple of hounds.

Hurrah! see he faces the Commons of Carney,
Whose broad and deep bound-drain says, none of your
    blarney,
But over, hark over! like hawks on the wing,
Horse and hound on the sod settled down to the thing.

When a scene right before us, for beauty we spy
To be imag'd alone on a foxhunter's eye;
The dogs that had split, have now flank'd the half-score,
In a chain all abreast—yards two hundred, or more.

For unwilling to tail, and unable to head it,
Instinct whisper'd, my beauties, keep running on credit,
Till thro' windings and hollows, as on swept the chase,
Not a hound of the pack but fell into his place.

And now we top walls we'd have cran'd at before,
While our huntsman (the second) sings out to Rossmore,
What's at your side, my lord? and look'd rather abroad,
When his lordship slued round, and said, I am, thank
    God!

Leaving Carrig-a-gown for the Peterfield woods,
Such a storm burst upon us! the rain fell in floods;
The boughs crash'd around, hurtled at us the hail,
But the pack kept their pace in the teeth of the gale!

Though with earths open here, the fox gallantly ran on,
Will Mr. O'Shinnach* make over the Shannon?

* Sionnach, Irish for fox.

No, he changes his mind, and now heads for Clough-
  prior,
And across the big drain of the loch, in the mire.

Of which, I am sorry to leave Burton Persse,
Disappearing, in all senses, by his reverse ;
I'll ne'er see that sweet face again, bellow'd Tony,
As, on ! was the word for the tow'r of Ardcrony.

You're wrong ; he's at home in that sort of a thing,
He's a Knight of the Bath, says the Colonel, by jing ;
Sure enough in a capital place, rode unhurt on,
As if for his cold bath the better, young Burton.

On, many a mile, through the old Castle ground,
And homeward, at length, bounding over the Bound !
For Reynard began, in his sorrow and pain,
To think, Will I see Coolaghgoran again ?

Game varmint ! his life we were willing to leave him,
But what could we do ? the Life-guards wouldn't save
  him ;
Old Winner, you see, is too close at his brush—
And so ended this chase, or this race, or this rush.

Twenty-five Irish miles ; one slight check thro' it all,
You may guess that the gay field at finding, grew small ;
With the hounds were George Jackson, Rossmore,
  Colonel Eyre,
Dick Falkiner, and Persse, thro' this furious affair ;

The Fitzgibbons, and Westenra, who, running in at
The death, took a jump which a light-weight a minute
Craned over, and swore 'twas the ugliest leap !
Though a nice place to shelter a large flock of sheep.

And now that I've shown what a play could perform
Colonel Eyre, and his pack, in the teeth of a storm;
Lower Ormond, farewell! and long may we remember
Eighteen hundred and nine, and the fourth of December!

GREEK EPIGRAM—LEONIDAS.

MARS SPEAKS.

Not mine these spoils! who offers at the shrine
   Of Ares, gifts, that wear such graceless grace?
Unruffled crests, and bucklers trim, that shine
   From blood-fleck free; unsplintered spear and mace.
The sweat of shame, while crimson dyes our face,
   Starts on the brow, down-dropping o'er the breast;
Away! and trick with these light things we scorn,
Some hall, or chamber for a bridal-morn;
   Spoils of the bloody goad befit us best,
Gory, and grim—let such our shrine adorn!

TO MY UNCLE.

Oh! thou, of relatives most kind,
Thee did I ne'er forgetful find,
Of little pledges left behind,
            My Uncle!

For all my clothes, however drest,
From hat to shoe, for coat and vest,
Who takes the highest interest?
            My Uncle.

While Victor Hugo hymns his brats,
And Cowper lauds his hares, or cats—
I only spout to one—and that's
            My Uncle.

Oh say, ye poor, when others shun ye,
Who never shuts—both doors—upon ye?
But keeps your duds, and lends ye money?
　　　　　My Uncle.

Whither shall harass'd Virtue flee,
Or Genius steep'd in poverty,
To find their duplicates? to thee,
　　　　　My Uncle.

The beauty's pearl, the soldier's sword,
The lover's fondly-treasured hoard,
Ev'n wedding-rings, with thee are stor'd,
　　　　　My Uncle!

Oh! never may I see the day,
When Mathew Barrington shall lay
Low 'neath his Mont de Pieté,
　　　　　My Uncle!

JOHN WALDRON.

Gay, gallant, gen'rous, simple, and sincere;
Sway'd by no hollow hope, no faithless fear;
While emulous in straining for the goal,
Without a shade of envy on his soul,
Here lies John Waldron! Carve upon the stone,
A man less selfish none have ever known.

One hour, how full of life!* The next he lay,
Resolving swiftly into kindred clay!
He pass'd away in his meridian hour,
Not yet the bloom had faded from the flow'r;
Not yet had cold congeal'd, or heat dried up
The dew-drop, gleaming in its calyx-cup;
Hope beckon'd still her rainbow to pursue,
And woman still was kind, and man seem'd true.

* This fine young man was accidentally shot.

Much wert thou miss'd in ev'ry manly sport;
Thy rush impetuous through the racket-court,
That looks a lonely dungeon, blank and bare,
Thy joyous shout no longer echoes there!
Miss'd at the hunters' meet, and in the chase,
A forward rider, whatsoe'er the pace;
But most I miss thee, on each lake and shore,
Where we have thrown a fly, or pull'd an oar,
Or clamber'd with our guns the mountain steep,
Or clear'd the bog-drain, oft so wide and deep,
To me, scarce hoping for the further side,
Thy hearty cheer unwonted strength supplied.
It were too sacred ground to touch upon
Their grief, who miss'd the brother, and the son!

Yet who can say, that with the world hath fought,
The change a few brief summers might have brought?
The doubt of friends, the ever-gnawing care,
The body's weariness, the heart's despair;
Thou might'st have liv'd, perhaps, to feel how vain
Is life, and left it after years of pain:
All this hast thou escap'd, by the same blow
That laid thy youthful aspirations low;
Perchance in haven on some happier shore,
While we are mourning thee, as if no more,
Thy spirit, wav'ring 'twixt a smile and tear,
Looks down on those condemn'd to linger here!

EPITAPHIUM CATHARINÆ TEXEÆ, AURELIENSIS.

Reader, art thou fain to know
What lies buried here below?
That I willingly would show,

If the greatest sage could tell,
What the name befits it well,
Sleeping in its narrow cell.

Might we judge by outward frame,
We should grant its virgin claim;
Yet a woman, can we name

That, which none have ever seen
Anxious look, or unserene,
Though the fates have adverse been?

In prosperity ne'er proud,
When it should be silent, loud;
Mute, when truth should be avow'd?

Ne'er the wanton dance to share,
Nor with robe, or hue, or hair,
The Madonna might not wear?

Never known with painted dyes,
Doubtful tongue, or ogling eyes,
Soul or body in disguise?

'Twas a man, we might opine
Could we disbelieve our eyne,
That sweet form is feminine!

'Twas some goddess then, of old,
Female-form'd, but manly-soul'd,
Pallas, such as poets told.

But of blood she bore a stain;
Of the others what they feign,
Chaster woman would disdain!

What is left, but to assume
Something lies within this tomb,
Above or man, or maid, or god of Heathendom!
Poemata juvenilia, THEODORI BEZÆ.

GREEK EPIGRAM ON A VINE.

PHILIPPUS.

What desolate unsunn'd nook, in sterile mould,
  Rear'd thee, wild vine? was't boreal Scythia's sod?
Or Celtic snow-struck Alp, aye pinch'd with cold;
  Or rude Iberia's iron-yielding clod?

Mother of clusters harsh, unmellow'd fruit,
  Weeping sour drops, in lieu of nectar fine;
Oh! for thy hands, Lycurgus, from its root
  To hew and hale this verjuice-bearing vine!

LE ROI D'YVETOT.

BERANGER.

In Yvetôt once, a king kept state,
  But little known to story,
Who lay down early, got up late,
  And never dream'd of glory,
Though crown'd by Jenny, it is said,
With cotton night-cap on his head,
      Abed.
Ho-ho, ha-ha! ho-ho, he-he!
What a good little king was He!
      He-he!

Four meals a day suffice his grace
 Within his well-thatched palace;
And on a Donkey, pace-a-pace,
 He through his empire dallies,
Gay, simple, credulous; yet how!
A royal guard salutes him now—
     Bow-wow!

His fiscal drain was drought, alas!
 Yet still to keep him sappy,
Oh, would grudge a king his glass,
 That made his people happy!
And so he levied, on the spot,
From ev'ry pipe his royal pot—
     Why not?

With maids of honour it was found
 His ways were winning rather;
And subjects oft had real ground
 To hail him as a father.
Four times a year his forces strut,
And fire away at nothing—but
     A butt.

He sought not for a neighbour's states,
 By aggrandizing measures;
And, pattern of all potentates,
 Compos'd his code of pleasures,
'Twas only when their monarch died,
His people sad, the grave beside,
     E'er cried.

They show the portrait of this Prince,
 So fam'd for worth and bounty,
The sign-board of the best of inns,
 Still noted in the county;

And often still, on holidays,
  The mob, with most admiring gaze,
                    Huzzas—
Ho-ho! ha-ha! ho-ho! he-he!
What a good little King was He,
                    He-he!

FROM BERANGER.

Bless thee, miserable Wine!
Ne'er wilt thou hurt me, or mine;
Let some better diner-out
Smack his lips at ev'ry bout;
O'er my plate besprinkle now
Scentless flow'rs, and dead, as Thou!
But—for health, when here I dine,
Bless thee, vapid, mawkish wine!

For—a bouquet didst thou boast,
Soon my memory were lost,
And the Doctor's warning too—
Cupid is enough for you;
Sing of Bacchus then, as do
Priests of gods they never knew;
But—for one dear girl of mine,
Bless thee, execrable Wine!

For, could stuff like thee inspire me,
That old Spanish flame might fire me;
If the little black-ey'd pirate
Fix'd my ransom at a high rate,
How Lisette, who keeps the budget
Of our ways and means, would grudge it!
But, thoul't ne'er make hearts beat quicker,
Bless thee, dead and damnéd liquor!

For, if thou couldst imp my pen,
Armed with pointed verse again,
Singing, reeling, I might smother
Some poor little King, or other;
Then I should be clapp'd in prison
And my fun be christen'd, Treason!
But—o'er thee, I feel a dastard,
Bacchus' most abortive bastard!

For in gaol there's little laughing;
But the wine I was not quaffing,
Disappears; and to my throttle
Now appeals a nectar bottle.
Fill a brimmer, I will toss over
Fear with it like a philosopher;
Fill again! I brave all danger;
Welcome, welcome, lovely stranger!

AMERICAN ADVERTISEMENT.

Whereas, my slave Joseph, has just ran away,
For what reason I challenge Columbia to say;
And I doubt if the fellow has one of his own,
Thank God my humanity's pretty well known;
Reward—dollars two hundred for Joe, or if dead—
Shoot him, should he resist you—a score for his head.
Said Joe may be known, if you come on his track,
By the wheals of the cowhide quite fresh on his back;
Look sharp near Squash Creek—his wife sold there,
    last Fall—
Application to Christian Love, Liberty Hall.

SLAVE LYRIC.

What may yon dark column be,
Marching slow through Tennessee?
Two and two, all mutely, men,
Women walking, children then;
Joyous anthems sung before them,
Starry banners waving o'er them—
" Hail Columbia! Happy land!"
What and whence the dusky band?

For I hear no merry din
Voicing to the violin;
For the men look worn and weary,
Women, children, sad and dreary;
For betwixt the double rank,
Sounds a curious sort of clank;
What can this dark column be,
Wending slow through Tennessee?

Stranger, those are hapless Slaves!
Freedom's banner o'er them waves;
And you hear the nation's song
Flouting Heav'n and that sad throng—
Ev'ry step the Negro strains,
Counted by the clank of chains;
What are ye, who buy or breed him?
Christians, stranger, sons of Freedom!

THOUGHT.

Friendship, with the wicked made,
Shortens, like the morning shade,
　　　Quickly ceasing;
With the good, its hallowed lines
Lengthen, as life's sun declines,
　　　Still increasing.

THE SOLDIER'S WIDOW.

FROM THE FRENCH OF MR. LEPEE.

The autumn was ended, and winter begun—
  November had hobbled half over;
And languid and dull at the slights of the sun,
  Earth pin'd like a girl for her lover.

Night was closing her dark wings; afar in the vale,
  One hut made the waste look more lonely,
The Angelus just had rung out, and the gale
  Brought the bell's dying dirge of it only.

A woman was slowly descending the hill,
  Her tear-swimming eyes turn'd to Heav'n;
She pray'd to our Mother of Sorrows, and still
  She cried, Lady dear, if it were but His will,
  That the children be spar'd and forgiv'n!

On her back, in the rags of what once was a cloak,
  An infant girl hung; her young brother
Lagg'd afoot, and grew sadder although he ne'er spoke,
  With the sighs that fell fast from his mother.

Poor boy, he strove hard not to cry that sore night,
  For soldiers ne'er did so, one told him,
With a smile beyond tears, on the eve of the fight—
  Never more shall a father enfold him!

Yet often he stole at his mother a look,
  As his poor little limbs grew more weary;
But his eyes soon fell back on the path they forsook,
  For her silence was even more dreary!

'Twas dark, and he then felt her hand on his head—
   That's a good boy; keep up, God will hear us;
We may yet get a crust for our supper, she said,
   And some straw, for a village is near us.

They reached it too late; all relief was denied,
   No one rose, not a candle was lighting;
My children are starving, she plaintively cried,
   For his country their father died fighting.

In vain, wretched mother, thy cries were in vain!
   Ev'ry door was close barr'd, while inside it
Men slept, or pretended to sleep, while thy pain
   The half-waken'd echoes derided.

Behind the last arch of an old Gothic church,
   The moon sank, her sad crescent gleaming
O'er some blackening thatch, and a ruinous porch,
   Like a Saint's eye on bed of death beaming.

Free inn of the traveller, home of the poor,
   There once the mere wretch hope might cherish;
Its sign, a small Crucifix over the door—
   'Twas the cot of the priest of the parish.

But when priests went erewhile out of fashion in France,
   Its late owner found death, but no grave!
While the village-child dar'd not show grief by a glance,
And the widow and orphans now sank on its transe,
   For the first time with no one to save.

Ah, my children 'tis over, and hope must now cease
   In this world; but God is above us;
We'll creep to the church-door; I'll pray on my knees,
That we all may soon meet in the other at peace,
   Where your father is waiting to love us.

Feeble sobs and deep groans rose amid the grave-stones,
  Christ Jesu! some deaths seem too bitter!
But their agony pass'd, as thine own, at the last—
  The rising sun shed a gay glitter,

O'er the ghastly scene where starvation had been,
  And a farmer, who in the night gave them
Deep curses, because they disturb'd him, I ween,
  Now ran, and, ha, ha! tried to save them!

THE BABY.

VICTOR HUGO.

When the Baby is brought, how the family-circle
Clap their hands and cry out, how the dimmest eyes
  sparkle,
    Its sparklers to see!
While the saddest brow there, the most ruffled
  perchance,
Grows smooth in the light of that small creature's
  glance,
    And its innocent glee!

Whether June deck my door,* or November illume
With a huge flick'ring fire the old family room,
  Our chairs touching all;
When Baby appears, oh what laughs and " sweet
  dears !"
As it toddles and stops, while its fond mother fears,
  That the darling will fall.

* Alludes to a large tree at the door of Victor Hugo's house
in Paris.

R.

We oft converse gravely, while stirring the fire,
On God and our country; of bards who aspire
  Bible-prophets, o'er Earth;
But the Baby in view, heav'n and country, adieu!
Sainted poets good bye! serious comments on you,
  Metamorphos'd to mirth!

At night when men sleep, but my fancy awakes,
And lists while the murmuring brook to the brakes
  Its sad story tells;
When the first hue of dawn like a pharos appears,
What a Babel of sound, what a hubbub one hears—
  Birds, insects and bells!

My soul seems the plain, and my infant the morn,
And perchance passing over its breath may have borne
  Some fragrance away;
Or my soul is the forest—all darkling it grieves,
Till Spring wakes the turtle-doves coo in its leaves,
  And gilds it with day!

For those eyes such an essence of gladness distil,
And those dear little hands, that have never done ill,
  May they be so when old!
On the mud of this earth thy twin feet never trode,
Thou fair-hair'd young child, thou fresh cherub of God
  With thy halo of gold!

The dove of our ark is that infant in white,
With feet so unsullied, and wings out of sight,
  Folded up, I am sure,
It peers on the world, wond'ring what it may mean,
In a double virginity, body all clean,
  And spirit all pure!

What it says mama knows, and the nurse—none beside;
Bless its credulous smile, and its tears swiftly dried,
    When ought goes amiss,
As it gazes about, from the sky to the ground,
And opens its soul out to nature around,
    And its mouth—for a kiss!

May heav'n save us all, mine own household, and those
Whom I love as dear friends, whom I pity, as foes,
    In their gall and their foam,
From a summer, without the bird's song in the trees,
From a spring without flow'rs, from the hive void of bees,
    From a babyless home!

THE LIAR.

FROM KIND.

Pat, of the Eighty-eighth, one day,
Fell, wounded, in a hot melée;
A comrade freed him, rais'd his head;
Tim, said the Captain, is he dead?
By my sowl, is he, sir. No, I'm not, mutter'd Pat;
    Tim then look'd as grave as a friar;
Captain dear, it's a pity we can't swallow that;
    But the poor boy was always a liar!

FROM GELLERT.

A father leaving his two sons forever,
John, rather dull, and Sidney, very clever;
Feeling himself about to die,
On Sidney gaz'd with sadden'd eye,
Thou hast such wit, my boy, sigh'd he;
What on earth will become of thee?
I have not much I can call mine,
But here's a casket with some coin;

Receive it then, my hapless son,
But mind to give your brother—none!
Sidney long star'd in dubious pother;
What will be left for John, my brother,
If I should keep all this, he said;
Oh! gasp'd the father, nearly dead,
My soul—is easy—about John;
A stupid fellow—he'll get on!

THE DIFFERENCE.

KIND.

A woman once conjur'd the prince, in vain,
To give her son, a conscript, back again.
"The state requires his arm," he said; "beside
That he's a soldier, should excite your pride.
Deem you a soldier then, so vile or common?
I am a prince, the king's my brother,
Yet we are soldiers, one and t'other."
"Because you knew no better," said the woman,
Whose patience now began to fail her;
"But my Tom serv'd his time, and is a tailor!"

INCIDENT ON THE MARCH OF AMERICAN
DRAGOONS.

Hurrah, my brave boys! The red river is pass'd,
The Arkansas is near, and Fort Riley at last!
After marching and hunting, how sweet to recline
"In the shade of our Shumac!"* to rest, and to dine,
Then to sleep with a saddle to pillow each head,
The horsecloth a blanket, the earth for a bed.
In a dream friends afar oft will fancy evoke,
And faces of home seem to smile through the smoke!

* Shumac—American—a species of tobacco.

Till the bugle recalls to our route fast and far,
And the buffalo-chase, fainter image of war;
For the herds are so num'rous, as sport we now cull
The wild prairie-monarch, the buffalo-bull;
We laugh at his gait so uncouth, yet soon find
That rude canter will leave us, if careless, behind.
But three miles have fatigued one who half scorns to run,
He now stands at bay, and the battle's begun;
Head down, mane erect, and tail lashing his side,
By heav'n, that grim bull, in his pow'r and his pride,
Were worth crossing th' Atlantic a moment to see;
Ware all! For he rushes—at you, or at me?
A miss is as good as a mile; we retire
Some paces, and pour in a fast-dropping fire;
Thirty balls thro' his hide, of which twelve in his skull,
We told on the death of that buffalo-bull!
Alas, for him now! He no longer will rove
Through the prairie, of many an Ino the Jove!
'Mid the flash and report, 'mid the shout and the smoke,
He meets death mute and firm as the thunderstruck oak.
Ha, he's down—he is dead; no, he staggers again
To his feet, shakes his neck with its wild-tossing mane,
And while inward and outward his ebbing veins gush,
Collects all his life for a desperate rush;
Wo worth the good horse that was tardy to turn,
He is ripp'd at one tear from his stem to his stern!
And the Buffalo-bull falls aveng'd by his side,
The prairie's brave monarch, he liv'd, and he died!

ON THE DERIVATION OF ALFANA FROM EQUUS.

D'ACEILLY.

Alfana comes from Equus, do you say;
A wond'rous change of horses by the way!

SONNET.

FROM THE ITALIAN.

By the dark robe, and stealthy footfall, lo,
  How near it comes!　And by those livid eyes,
  And ashy lineaments, I recognise
My summoner; I will not say, my foe.
My spirit loathes its tangled tendrils so,
  The scythe that sweeps them off, I may despise,
  Yea, welcome, since it severs not the ties
To Him, from whom futurity must flow.
Man, born in tears, here lingers day by day,
  An exile from his native land outlaw'd,
    Groping thro' grief and darkness toward his goe
Welcome, dark messenger! ah, why delay
    The stroke, that promises my weary soul
Eternal peace, re-union with its God!

EPIGRAM.

D'ACEILLY.

Dido tells ev'ry one she knows I love her;
Though this I was not able to discover,
I cannot think of contradicting Dido;
For faith she knows a great deal more than I do.

THE MOURNFUL TOURNEY.

UHLAND.

Sev'n noble barons spur apace,
  And shield and spear they bring,
A tourney good they hold, to grace
  The daughter of their king.

They heard, when near the castle-wall,
  A tinkling bell inside,
And when they trode the kingly hall,
  Sev'n tapers lit they spied.

And lying there, sweet Adelaide,
  Pale on her bier, and mild;
The monarch sitting at her head,
  And weeping o'er his child.

Thereon, spoke haughty Dagobert,
  Forever must I mourn,
That all in vain my steed I've girt,
  And shield and spear up-borne.

Then young Sir Atheling broke forth,
  We'll waste on that no tear;
The daughter of the king's aye worth
  A thrust of sword or spear!

Sir Walter spake, a soldier keen,
  To horse, and home, quoth he;
Small guerdon gives the joust I ween,
  When for a dead ladye!

Cried Atheling, what if she's dead?
  There lives no maid so fair!
A guerdon rich, her roses red,
  And ring of gold, to wear!

Then forth they gallop'd to the plain,
  Those noble Ritters sev'n,
And sore the strife, till six remain
  With faces turn'd to heav'n.

The seventh, Sir Atheling, rode on,
　The vanquisher of all;
But weary from his steed, and wan,
　He trode the kingly hall.

He wore her wreathe of roses red,
　Her ring of gold, and fell
Upon the daïs, stark and dead,
　By her he lov'd so well.

The king is clad in weeds of woe,
　The bells toll far and wide,
For six good knights, that lay full low,
　Interr'd in pomp and pride.

The seventh was young Sir Atheling,
　By Adelaide, his own;
The fresh cool earth their covering,
　Beneath a single stone.

PARODIED FROM SCHILLER'S
"DISTRIBUTION OF THE EARTH."

Among ye be it, boys; I leave the earth;
　Though I'm not going to die, I make an heir,
Said Jove, of ev'ry man of you, at birth;
　Provided always—he can get his share.
Then if men had a hundred hands apiece,
　They'd be too few to scramble with that day,
The farmers grabb'd potatoes, corn, and geese,
　The fowlers at the coveys blaz'd away.

The fishers took the salmon, trout, and cods;
　The friars laid in the whiskey, fowl, and chine;
The king clapp'd turnpikes upon all the roads,
　With "Please pay here; no trust upon this line."

Ochone, too late, when each had made his haul,
   Up walks the poet, like the devil-may-care;
But wirrastrue, he got no place at all,
   Because there was a tenant ev'rywhere.

Oh Jove! and me alone, your singing-bird;
   To leave me out! oh, murder, me alone!
With such a screech as heav'n had never heard,
   He flung himself, and lay like a big stone.
If you were dreaming of queer fairy-places,
   Says Jove, why, don't be aggravating me!
Where on earth were you, when they got the leases?
   Why, says the poet, where then would I be,

But up in heav'n? at such a splendid sight,
   When fairly bother'd, and such songs, and speakers,
To fall out with me you have little right,
   If I forgot about the dirty acres.
Walker! said Jove, and took a pinch of snuff;
   I've parted with the earth, my poor old buck;
But you are welcome here, and that's enough;
   So make yourself at home, and take pot luck!

THE RICHEST PRINCE.

FROM THE GERMAN.

Erst at Worms their rich dominions
   Vaunting loud with rival strain,
In the Kaisar-hall were quaffing
   Peers and princes of Almaine.

Quoth the Saxon Count, how glorious,
   My land, in, or out of sight!
With its beauteous mountains hoarding
   Silver veins, like solid light!

Lo! my princedom steep'd in plenty,
  Cried th' Elector of the Rhine,
Golden ears in all its vallies,
  On its heights the purple vine.

Then spoke Louis of Bavaria,
  Wealthy abbeys, cities wide,
Need a realm that owns such riches
  Yield to any land beside?

Eberhard, the snowy-bearded,
  Wurtemburg's belovéd lord,
Said, my home hath no large city,
  And its hills no silver hoard.

Yet doth it contain a treasure
  Thro' its woods, roam where I please,
This old head in sleep were pillow'd
  Safely on a subject's knees.

Shouted then the lordly Saxon,
  They of Bayern and the Rhine,
Bearded Count, thou art the richest,
  Thou dost own a diamond-mine!

EPIGRAM.

D'ACEILLY.

Joseph mourns above all things
His father's *tedious* sufferings;
Some say Joseph's grief is rather
For his father's son than father.

THE DIVISION OF THE EARTH.

SCHILLER.

Take freely, as I give it; take the earth,
    Cried Jove from high; be man henceforth my heir;
His title shall be good by right of birth,
    But, brother-like, let each one have a share.
Then the two-handed race to grasp and gain,
    They hurried, young and old, without delay;
The farmer seiz'd the fields of golden grain,
    To wood and wold the hunter bent his way.

The merchant stores the goods his ships deliver,
    The abbot revels on the racy wine;
The king block'd up the bridge, the road, and river,
    And tribute, tax and toll, he said, are mine.
When all was shar'd, too late, alas! drew nigh
    The poet from afar, with wilder'd brow;
O'er the wide earth no spot could he descry
    To call his own; each hath a landlord now.

Ah me, shall I alone, your truest child,
    Forgotten be? of all, but I alone!
So, with a wailing cry, both shrill and wild,
    He flung himself before the thund'rer's throne.
If thou through visionary realms wert faring,
    Replied the god, lay not the blame on me!
Where wert thou all this while the earth was sharing?
    With thee, the poet cried; I was with thee!

Upon thine aspect raptur'd hung my sight,
    Still in my ear thy voice celestial rings;
Forgive my spirit, dazzled by such light,
    That it forgot all low, and earthly things.
What help? said Jove; the earth is mine no more;
    Chase, farm, hill, plain, stream, all away are giv'n;
But when thou wilt, come hither as before,
    Enjoy my countenance, and share my heav'n!

SORROW'S SON.

FROM THE SWEDISH.

Upon the lonely ocean strand
  Sate Sorrow, turn'd from heav'n away,
And moulded with a careful hand
  A human likeness out of clay.

Jove comes; What is it, doth he ask;
  Great sire, 'tis but a piece of earth,
Yet to thy power an easy task
  To gift it with a spirit birth.

Live then! But subject to my yoke,
  As compensation for the loan;
Nay, Sorrow with a shriek out-broke,
  Nay, do not take my child, my own!

By me hath he been shadow'd forth,
  Yea, but his life by me was giv'n;
As thus they strove, pass'd mother Earth
  Beheld the shape, and, King of Heav'n!

From me, from out my breast, she cried,
  This stolen form I here reclaim!
Well, Saturn shall the cause decide,
  And Saturn's judgment who shall blame?

Let none repine—such was his doom—
  This image doth to all belong;
Jove gave him life, and can resume,
  And yet no other suffer wrong.

Thou, Earth, receive his bones; fulfil
    Thy mission at his death, in peace;
But Thou, his mother, sorrow, still,
    With life alone, thy claim shall cease.

From thee thy Son until his end
    Shall not be sever'd, ev'n a day;
Thy sighs shall with his being blend;
    Thy features model ev'ry trait.

Almighty fate the Sentence gives;
    And, Man, submissive to its code,
Belongs to Sorrow, while he lives,
    But when he dies, to Earth and God.

DANTE.

ON THE DEATH OF BEATRICE.

Ah, pilgrims, wending with a pensive gait,
    Your thoughts perchance on things that are not here,
    From such a distant clime do ye appear,
As your calm countenances indicate?
For thro' our city in its mourning state
    Ye pass along the streets, yet shed no tear,
    Like persons who feel neither doubt nor fear,
Nor understanding of our grievous fate,
    But if your course, to learn it ye defer,
My heaving heart can read you at what cost;
    Those eyes unwet no longer will ye keep!
For pilgrims, know, its Beatrice is lost—
    And words that any one can speak of Her,
Possess a virtue to make others weep.

GARDEN.

LEONORA—TASSO.

Leo. Torquato, thou'rt a bookworm; hast thou read
How a king lov'd a beggar; canst recal
The names?
    Tasso.   Cophetua, madam, was the king's;
The beggar's*—I've forgotten.
    Leo.   Hardly fair
The pretty gypsy! Was Cophetua crazed?
    Tasso. He was in love.
    Leo.   Is love, then, lunacy?
    Tasso. Most genealogists count them akin;
Yet in my poor mind, madam, the insane
Do only love themselves, or rarely dote
Too fondly on another.
    Leo.   Yet, Torquato,
'Twas a strange choice!
    Tasso.   In fortune, not in him.
He had no choice; he could not choose but love;
He trembled at the voice of that poor girl,
Against his will, and blush'd before a beggar!
Doubtless his pride was wounded deep; he thought
On all the mocks and jibes, the leers and winks
Among the fine court ladies—all that pass'd;
And love look'd on, and smil'd to see his struggles
'Gainst pride and prudence, and a host beside.
Then first Cophetua found upon this earth
A heav'n—'twas in his *heart;* he lov'd another;
And what to her was all the world beside?
How sweet existence grew! Forgive me, lady,
I meant to say, the girl—that is, the king—
May not have been so very lunatic.
    Leo. Nay, Tasso, trust me he *was* phrenetic;

* Penelophon.

May heav'n preserve our wits ! His story seems
To breathe contagion, for your eye and cheek,
So quiet late and cool, grew feverish
In telling it : the sparkle and the flush,
Have scarcely left them yet; oh, good Torquato,
Beware such gypsy girls, and so, farewell ! *Exit.*

    Tasso (alone). She flouts me with her lips, yet oft her
      eye
Beams moon-like on my tossings; she doth err—
I am not mad; or if, yet not so mad
As to believe in ballad, or romance,
Of poets wooing princesses—nor dreamt,
Save once, that e'er I kissed—and then I woke,
Affrighted at my great audacity,—
The topmost roundlets of her taper hand.
It is enough to be where she hath been,
To syllable her tones, recall her looks,
And people solitude with one sweet shape.
As long as fate shall leave such memories,
I can dispense with hope, too faintly known
To be much miss'd ; a kind of distant cousin,
On whose decease we say, Aye, all must die !
Must we all die ? our bodies must—our souls ?
Can spirit perish ?   If it came from nought,
Why may not it return ?   A deathless Name—
Is that a sound, a dream, and nothing more ?
Will Homer be forgotten or his songs,
That seem to have secur'd, while language lasts,
At least an earthly immortality ?
All men live in their works, or in their offspring,
If few in name ; shall I survive in either ?
Shall Tasso's name be echoed from the shores
Of far off lands, while beauty cons his page,
And sighing, links that name, with—Leonora's ?

There is a class of men lead double lives ;

One, real and apparent, as 'tis called;
The other in a higher spirit-land.
The Earth-shine here, compared with that, shows dim,
Cold, wearisome; and thus the one-lived men
Eye them suspiciously, and style them strange.
This irks them, like the long-lost traveller,
Who but returns to home, to find all chang'd:
So if he leave it not, he mingles with it
Snatches of foreign scene, and other tongues;
Misunderstood—deem'd mad, and soothly too,
If it be wise to fret out life for gold,
A bauble, or a ribbon—or a—woman.
If it be wise to scorn the Actor's art,
That pictures forth the poet's bright ideas,
To call some great Musician, fool, or fiddler:
To shut the eye, and bar the ear to all
Save money, self, and sensuality;
To yawn o'er names that gem the night of Time;
To feel no sympathy with patriots,
With martyrs none; to wrap up all in self,
Including our dear wife and family,
And nothing else admire; if this be wisdom,
Some men are mad—and Tasso, most of all!

Oh how my thirsty childhood drain'd in Naples,
Long draughts of honied lore, while rev'rend men
Of Jesu's brotherhood, who gave the cup,
Smil'd on their eager nursling; listen'd mild
To his verse-lispings, and the eloquence
Of nine years old, and marvel'd at his growth.
Then boyhood came, and spake with other tongues
Than that a mother taught; nay, rather laugh'd,
And coo'd, and kiss'd within my infant lips.
Then learn'd I willingly from Cattaneo,
Most fortunate in him, how Homer sang,
And Plato spoke, and Sappho sigh'd to love.

The Latin, too, the echo of Hellenic,
That seems to sigh in dirges of the past;
The 'Fuimus' to us of Italy!
Twelve years brought graver studies; Padua
Held forth theology and either law,
And all nam'd love of wisdom by the Greek.
In all the laurel crown'd my thoughtful brow;
Thoughtful at sev'nteen summers, ah too soon
For smile serene at threescore years and ten.
I have liv'd fast in soul, and now methinks
Am growing old; the scabbard will not lag,
God grant at least it may not, long behind
As I do sometimes dread, the worn-out weapon!
Oh, those young days! Then dawn'd a witching form,
Fairer than woman's, on my reveries,
When I grew ripe for love; I wooed it long,
Nor know if I have won thee, Poesy!
From many a rival of my age and clime;
Yet have I hope, nay, more, a confidence,
That Tasso's suit to thee was not in vain—
I shall *not* be forgotten!

FROM THE GERMAN.

Two worlds I love; the third I fain would shun;
At calm, clear eve, I wistful gaze on one,
   Whence peer the beauteous stars, with watching pale;
One is beneath; thine home, eternal Night!
No hope is there, no wonder, nor delight;
   There shines no star, there sighs no gentle gale.

Why wakes this Third fair world nor smile, nor tear!
Aye, probe my heart! Alas, she is not here,
   Who made me capable of such, with love:
Deep, in the silent grave, her body lies;
Her spirit wing'd its way to Paradise;
   I too would fain lie low, or soar above.

s

ODYSSEUS, AND THE SIRENS.

Oh stay, Odysseus, stay!
The Chief who sought not willingly the war,
For what to him was Troy,
Compar'd with his young wife and blooming boy?
  Will he now waste his latter life away,
In seeking what ev'n then he car'd not for,
  Vain honour, vainer gold on foreign strand?
Oh hero, far too wise to roam,
  Again would'st sow with salt the sand,
To find thy much chang'd home?
Telemachus is man-like; loves to reign,
  Thy wife hath wither'd from her early charms
Say, doth he wish a father back again,
  Or will Penelopé, within thine arms
Seem what she was ten years agone?
Or time restore thy lusty prime,
That while it lasted, seem'd to laugh at time?
  If so, then hurry on!
Nor seek with us beneath the waves,
Our pearl and coral caves,
With miracles beyond belief,
  And couches of the eider down,
Reserv'd for thee, oh prudent chief,
And favours, where no censors frown
  No laws forbid;
But for our beauty, if our forms seem fair,
  Let what thou viewest vouch for what is hid.
Yet have we gifts more rare,
Immortal offspring of the waters,
Than earth's imperfect short-liv'd daughters,

Who feed the grosser fire,
But leave in the etherial mind,
 Much to desire!
With them enjoyment ever grows more scant,
 And comprehensive spirits find
 A wistfulness and want,
Oh stay, Odysseus, stay!
 Where canst thou look for more than we can give?
 Not on a barren rock to live,
Or in some ballad to a future day,
 Is worthy thy transcendant merit,
No, but to spurn an earthly fate,
To find in Ocean home a deathless date,
 With goddesses; there to inherit
The wonders of another element,
Whose colour, form, and sound, and scent,
Surpass whatever thou hast known
As our expansive realm, thine own!
 From the sweet honey-gurgling mouth
The tones all mellow'd with the lyre,
Awaken'd such desire,
 They seized the hero with a spell
More than Circean; dreams of youth
 Breath'd from a rosy-tinted shell,
Mingled with spice-gales of the south;
 Their hair, eyes, bosoms, ecstasy intense;
 Intoxicating soul and sense!
He wrench'd in vain the cords,
 He shouted to his crew,
They saw his struggles, but they heard no words,
 What could Odysseus do?
Ah well for him that all his eloquence
 Forestall'd by wisdom, was in vain!
 Or Ithaca had seen him not again!
On sail'd the ship; he writh'd, he beat the deck
 With frantic feet; to Jove he pray'd,

And to the bright-eyed Maid,
At once the boat to wreck;
  Aye, though he perish in the deep,
  With those Sea-maids to sleep!
On swept the bark, the Sirens tore their hair,
Then div'd, and in despair
Left the once fatal shore,
And save in Memory's glass, were seen no more.

MODERN. GREEK SONG.

Bright Phosphor shed around his brilliant glance.
  Where Hellas' tented sons were lying lowly,
While near the camp, and brandishing his lance,
  The youthful Pelopídas* chanted slowly;
Oh fly at once ye Zephyrs, sweet and bland,
  And thro' lov'd Hellas let our brethren rally,
Say for the sake of fatherland,
Yes for thy fame my native land,
I watch by night within the valley,
I sing my night-song in the valley.

The war to-morrow's sun will soon awake,
  And valour's day will dawn; if, ere his setting,
For my dear country and sweet freedom's sake,
  Beside my spear I slumber, all forgetting;
Fly fly again, oh zephyrs soft and bland,
  Whisper lov'd Hellas, and each Grecian ally,
That for thy fame, oh fatherland,
Yes for thy glory, native land,
We fought and fell within the valley;
I slept in death down in the valley.

      * *Pelopídas,* modern Greek pronunciation.

FROM THE 18TH PSALM.

The Lord is my rock, and my bulwark, and tow'r;
The foe vaunted loud in the pride of his pow'r;
'Mid the sorrows of death, from the jaws of the grave,
I called upon Him who is mighty to save.

From his temple the cry of the wrong'd and the lone
Shot up through the seraphs that circle the throne,
He frown'd; heav'n grew black, as with smoke before
    fire,
While shudder'd pale earth at the thought of his ire.

He bow'd down the heavens, descending in might,
The cherubs his steed, his pavilion the night,
Thick clouds roll'd before him, dark waters behind,
As the Lord rush'd to war on the wings of the wind!

He spake, and it thunder'd; the clouds shrank away
Shrivel'd up in the blaze of unbearable day,
For the Lord but look'd forth, while it lighten'd around,
Where, where is the late haughty foe to be found!

The earth was dried up at the blast of thy breath,
Like the body of man at the bidding of death;
Its bones lying bar'd, as the waves turn and flee,
While their channels are trac'd in the depths of the sea.

The sorrows of hell on my spirit were laid,
The flood of ungodliness made me afraid;
But His hand was outstretch'd; I am sav'd to record
The goodness of God, and the might of the Lord!

FRENCH LADY ON ENGLISH TRAVELLERS.

How silent John Bull!
  Neither asks, nor replies;
If wise, he's a fool;
  If a fool, he is wise.

THE FAIR HILLS OF ERIN.

IRISH.

To Erin's lov'd land from my heart bear a blessing,
  Well-a-day and heigho!
And to Ir's race and Heber's, life there still possessing,
  Well-a-day and heigho!
The land made so sweet by the birds' tender tale,
Like the harp's slender strings keening sad for the Gael,
Oh, my grief, that a thousand miles sever my wail,
        From the fair hills of Erin, oh!

Soft and smooth are the heads of those hills with sweet
    fountains,
  Well-a-day and heigho!
And better than this land the worst of her mountains,
  Well-a-day and heigho!
Tall and straight are her trees, her woods level to tread,
With blossoms like lime on their bough-tops bespread,
There is love in my heart, and my thought-weary head,
        For the green hills of Erin, oh!

There are striplings in Erin, and those not a few,
  Well-a-day and heigho!
Troops of warriors in hundreds could ne'er conquer you,
  Well-a-day and heigho!
My heart's long affliction, my bitter lament,
'Neath the churl and the stranger in bondage ye're bent,
For the meted out fields ye must pay the high rent
        On the fair fields of Erin, oh!

Oh! many and mighty the ricks Erin makes,
    Well-a-day and heigho!
And the honey and cream there are flowing in flakes,
    Well-a-day and heigho!
I must go and see, if my life I would spare,
That dear little island the Gael ought to share,
Than the richest of ransoms, I'd rather be there,
        On the green hills of Erin, oh!

The dew gently sprinkles the corn-blades and grass there,
    Well-a-day and heigho!
And apple-bent branches smell sweet as you pass there,
    Well-a-day and heigho!
In glens of the mist do be sorrel and cress,
And the brooks summer-babble as daylight grows less,
Bright beauty and virtue the maidens possess,
        On the fair hills of Erin, oh!

A welcoming place and an open is Erin,
    Well-a-day and heigho!
Where a harvest of labour each grain-top is bearing,
    Well-a-day and heigho!
Of her cows and their calves, oh! far sweeter the lowing
Than fingers o'er musical chords nimbly going,
While on young and on old the bright sunbeams are
  glowing,
        O'er the green hills of Erin, oh!

WOMAN'S MISSION.

TO A LADY, WHO ACCUSED THE AUTHOR OF UNDERVALUING IT.

Woman's mission! Woman's mission,
If she knew her true position,

Would appear both very high, and very humble;
And if she wont agree
In the latter point with me,
  Soon or late her silly pride will have a tumble.

Man will find a loss to win her,
If she cannot dress his dinner,
  If his table have no fowl, flesh, or fish, on;
If she cannot keep her house,
Her babies, self, and spouse,
  Clean, and tidy—she knows little of her mission.

If she count not to a tittle
What she spends, or much or little,
  If she cannot darn and sow, and hem and stitch on,
If, with all her self-denial,
She expect not many a trial,
  Of her patience; well-a-day for her mission!

But such thraldom not required
By her state, were not desired
  In a lady of superior ambition;
And her twenty thousand pounds,
If her wretch don't take to hounds,
  May pay the ruder duties of her mission.

And more leisure let her find
To cultivate her mind,
  To mingle more Divine with the Human;
To appear in grace and worth,
Like a seraph sent on earth,
  And is she not, the darling gentlewoman!

Do you think I would not pet her,
Were she mine; oh yes, and let her

Ride and drive, and go to op'ras, balls, and races;
Or shoot with the long bow,
Attended, as we know,
  By Eros, and his Mother, and the Graces.

She might draw, and play, and study,
And yet not neglect the body,
  Its beauty and demeanour, dress and carriage;
And methinks it were as well
If fair Lady Bonnibelle
  Remain'd a " charming creature" after marriage.

I'd not leave her in the lurch,
Even when she went to church,
  Meeting, chapel, or whatever her religion;
My sweet parson, pope, and priest,
I'd attend to her at least,
  As Mohammed us'd to listen to his pigeon.

Yet most, methinks, I'd love her,
At the times when she would hover
  O'er thousand forms of suff'ring, shame, and sorrow,
When her presence might avail,
Like dear Florence Nightingale,
  For help to-day, and hoping for to-morrow.

But the wealthy, high, and gay,
Are the few, I grieve to say,
  The butterflies, in summer's bright pavilions;
And penury and gloom,
Are too often woman's doom,
  When we reckon up the slav'ry of the millions.

Mind and body, from her birth,
Chain'd to meanest wants on earth,

To ennoble ev'n the lowliest condition,
To train herself and others,
Husband, little ones, and brothers,
  For a better land, methinks, is woman's mission.

Felt and seen, far more than heard,
Oft before it finds a word,
  By her instinct to anticipate the wish on
Other lips, the while her own,
Dies unnoticed or unknown,
  Is woman's fate, self-sacrifice, and mission!

Do you deem such duties lowly?
They seem to me most holy;
  To me, indeed, they seem superhuman;
And I dream of sympathies
Dropping down from angel-eyes,
  In the gentle summer-rain, for such a woman.

Aye, methinks, they weep o'er all
The miseries that befal
  That creature, here oft tempted to perdition,
Who from Eden forc'd to roam,
Made a paradise of home,
  And smiling thro' her tears, own'd—her mission!

BYRON.

ON READING TRELAWNEY'S ACCOUNT OF HIS BODY.

Capricious, selfish, violent, and vain;
  Yet ever charitable, often kind,
    Though Nature's malice rankled in his mind,
That link'd him to deformity and pain.

No Pallas taught his boyhood to disdain
  The body's paltry doom; far less to find
  A gen'rous solace in the wish to bind
A neighbour's wounds; his mother, but his bane!
Poor Byron! Yet how rich the legacy
  Thy spirit did a wond'ring world bequeath,
  The poet's high atonement for the man!
How can we blame, how shall we pity thee,
  Oh! beauteous Torso, with the laurel wreath,
  Apollo all above, to end in Pan!

SONNET.

Star of the North, I bless thy looks of light—
  Not, that the Trader, thou didst lead full long,
  Or Warrior, o'er the wave, or Priest, to wrong
The native of some vainly-distant site,
Till then unconscious of black-hearted White,
  With prayer-book, liquid fire and bloody thong;
  For this, be still the cynosure of song.
To all, whom thou dost, trembling, guide aright,
That dusky Afric's Christian-captured son
  With glance upbraiding heav'n, eyes Thee afar,
(Is there a Slave who knows not, Thee?—Not one.)
  And thrills with hope, despite the chain and scar,
That where Thou beckonest, Freedom may be won,
  For this, I bless thy beams, Oh, Northern Star!

LINES TO THE MEMORY OF DR. HINCKS.

Pure, simple, unsuspecting as a child,
With learning, modest; and with virtue, mild;
Confiding in his own, he felt no need
To meddle with his Christian brother's creed.

No spot of earth too distant for his ken,
To him nought foreign of his fellow-men;
Their languages, or old or new, were known
Not for vain show, but to improve his own;
To teach the Western youth a classic style,
To light with Eastern lamp his native Isle,
And open wide the Book, that rates above
All tongues, what he was e'en more rich in—Love.
And mutual love to him gave many a pledge;
His was Paternity's best privilege—
The privilege of multiplying mind,
And in his race improving still his kind!
Lo, One who lifts the veil of centuries,
And reads Time's dimmest records at his ease,
Identifies the mummy with the man,
And shrinks Oblivion's kingdoms to a span.
Another, Nature has designed for sway,
By teaching men to rule, while they obey:
Equal to him, with thoughts of duty done,
Canadian ice, or bright Barbadian sun.
Then some who read in Nature's Bible, aw'd
Nought too minute to find, or vast for God;
And, bringing microscopic worlds to view,
May marvel such are known, or prized by few;
And some who bend their thoughts on Holy Text,
And make this life a preface to the next.
His daughters—but publicity they shun—
Self sacrifice and daughter-love are one,
Enough that his'for many a year could blend,
With that sweet name, the Nurse, Companion, Friend.
While thus, a true metempsychosis runs,
From worthy parent on in worthy sons,
Had Man no better-founded hope to Be,
Ev'n such were not mean Immortality!
  Farewell, old friend! not many days have flown
Since last my hand was clasp'd within thine own;

I felt the body's hold on human things,
But heard the rustling of the spirit's wings;
And, turning pensive from thy kindly door,
Farewell, I sighed—we meet on earth no more!

———

QUEEN'S VISIT TO IRELAND.

The Queen is coming—up, and out!
  Where can she best be seen?
Oh see the crowd, and hear their shout,
  Hurrah! she comes—the Queen!

A Lady in a chariot pass'd,
  Bow'd, smil'd, and glided on;
We make large eyes, and find at last
  Our tongues, when she is gone.

Her husband sitting by her side,
  Two graceful boys succeed;
No state, no scorn, no pomp or pride,
  Was that the Queen indeed?

Oh silly thoughts, 'tis worth a life
  To see what we have seen—
In such a mother, such a wife,
  The Woman hide the Queen!

All ceremony flung apart,
  Her guard, too, laid aside;
Wherever beats an Irish heart,
  My Guard is there, she cried.

Aye, Lady, tho' some hearts are riv'n
  For Exiles o'er the sea;
Not one contains a thought, by heav'n,
  To injure thine, or thee!

And safer than in London street,
  Or Windsor's tow'r ere while,
'Cead mile failte' will thou meet
  Throughout thine own Green Isle.

She walks, no diamonds on her brow,
  No sceptre in her hand,
That thousand-throng'd Pavilion now,
  The Lady of the land!

No diamonds!   What were then in Rome
  Cornelia's matchless gems?
Methinks our royal boys at home
  Worth scores of diadems!

What sceptre doth she need, to prove
  Her pow'r, who hath a charm
To lean upon a people's love,
  A husband's faithful arm!

She came, saw, conquered; marking well
  What Irish hands could do;
Eire-go-bragh, our cheering, swell!
  Victoria, abu!

LINES.

The mountain-maid, all witless how
  Her eyne would pierce me through,
Half arched her arm above her brow
  To shade those orbs of blue.

And as she stood with golden gleams
   Her golden hair upon,
She seem'd, embraced in his warm beams,
   The darling of the Sun!   .

On ev'ry thing around her glance
   Flitted a little space,
And then by chance, oh happy chance!
   Alighted on my face.

There what no tongue could ever speak,
   Yet love can spell, it found ;
And blushes mantled o'er her cheek—
   While sought her eyes the ground.

But how I woo'd, and how I won,
   Were idle sure to tell ;
What lover, since the world begun
   Deem'd any loved as well.

Ah little dream'd I, by thy side,
   Of days so dark as these,
My sunny-hair'd and summer-eyed—
   My early lost Louise!

EUTHANASIA.

Hark, the glad Bells ! the birthday of our Queen !
   London's vast hive thrills to the very core
   With life, and motion ; onward gaily pour
The younger groups, a twofold spring, I ween,
Careering through their veins ; while age is seen
   With quiet smile, contrasting forms of yore
   And this fantastic Now, where soon no more
Shall flit its own athwart the shadowy screen.

How much that Morn had Merivale enjoy'd,
　In his lov'd offspring's joy at sounds, and sights!
Then came the cheerful family-meal; and then,
As if to round the day without a void,
　The Scholar's calm and elegant delights;
Last came sweet Sleep—why should he wake again?

TO THE

MEMORY OF ROBERT BURNS.

A Century elaps'd, the Day returns,
That mark'd an Aloe, blossom, in a Burns.
More frequent blooms of late the Tree may shed,
More frequent Bards may slumber with the Dead;
That Century saw a Scott, a Campbell, claim
Room, ho! for Scotland, high on roll of Fame:
Saw England boast of Poets half a score,
And Ireland smile, and sigh, above Tom Moore.
Crabbe, Wordsworth, Southey, Coleridge, lo, they pass,
Keats, Shelly, Byron, o'er the Magic Glass,
While Memory sweeps off the breath of Time,
And Death gives back the beauteous and sublime;
But all not thine, dark king! while yet lives on—
Long may he live! our Alfred Tennyson.
Yet on this Constellation, look, and say,
Could one, or all, the loss of Burns repay?
Start not, oh Southern! Not indeed to you,
(For praise is irony, if more than due,)
But to a Nation of hard-handed men,
Who ill could want this Poet's Lyre, and Pen,
His words familiar, and his rustic style,
The broad and nervous Saxon of our Isle;
Who eye your bright and beautiful afar,
But fix their gaze upon the Northern Star!

To them, were Shakespeare, Milton, insecure,
Of fame undying; yet the Scottish poor,
Their Muse unheard, amid their daily toil,
'Neath skies inclement, on a sterile soil,
Were rich in Poetry—who read, by turns,
The Psalms of David, and the Songs of Burns!
Immortal songs! of Love, or Drink, or Fun,
But genial, heart-pervading, ev'ry one!
Contrast with such a Crabbe's ascetic tone,
Or smile sardonic, on a face of stone,
With his—who made each mode of humble life, his own!
His very Beggars, such a jolly crew,
That we half wish we had been beggars too.
How sweet with him to stray by rocks and rills,
Or spring, elastic, o'er the heath-clad hills!
To see the gowans glint by bonny Doon,
To hear the lav'rock lilting high aboon,
And feel our hearts, and Nature's, beat in tune!
Nor songs alone—the Bruce's battle-hymn,
The Wallace-wight, who looms in grandeur dim,
The Cotter's Sabbath-eve, and Christian's glory,
And Tam O'Shanter's jewel of a story,
Where, in Kirk-Alloway's strange corpse-lit aisle,
We scarce repress a shudder with our smile.
His satire, too, that ever seem'd to start
The verse-pour'd indignation of the heart;
What vice could hope from its keen shafts to flee,
When cow'ring low, uncloak'd hypocrisy,
'Neath his half-stern, half comical regard,
With rueful phyz, must own th' avenger bard?
Lo, now, what frolics and what "freits"* are seen
With lads, and lasses, on gay Hallowe'en!
That Vision last, in which a conscious worth,
How manly-modest, and how just, breaks forth!

* Freits—charms.

No self-appreciation e'er was grac'd
With more Refinement, Poetry, and Taste.
Oh, had Burns liv'd to hear each glorious deed,
When Highland Mary's clans rush'd on to bleed,
When far o'er Alma's heights was borne the cheer—
'We will hae nane but Hieland bonnets here!'
To India's sands, and Lucknow's leaguer'd walls,
Where one by one each hapless hero falls,
Till—can it be?   Hush!   Hear ye not yon strain?
The Campbells come!   And valor breathes again—
With what a glorious Pæan were they crowned!
And what a stream of song would set old Earth around!

But Bards by working-bees are often thought
A kind of Drones—half idle, and half naught.
In Burns, at least, no dreamer vain we see,
His Life was one too stern Reality;
Oh simple worldings, in his hard-worked hours
This Poet far surpass'd your highest pow'rs!
His wealth of soul unsumm'd, behold him now,
A stalworth peasant bending o'er his plough,
Toiling to feed his nestlings, and his mate,
With sweat-dew'd bread, begrudg'd by bitter fate;
Wet, weary, cold, late, early, see him swink
For coarsest clothing, lodging, food and drink!
Yet, as the Lark, its sky-ward road along,
Gladdens all nature with a gush of song,
So, from this Working-man, such lays had birth
As mingled gleams of heav'n with clods of earth;
To future generations joy to yield,
From him who traced his furrow in the field;
Wedding to heavy labour, lightsome verse;
And turning to a Boon, man's primal curse.

I tell ye, sorrowfully, if ye knew
The value of a soul, and what is due

To such a genius, from such clay as you,
This Day, in lieu of feasts and self-laudation,
Were a Black Fast of deep Humiliation!
In Scotland, chief—in England, weeds were worn
Of darkest dye, to mark the natal morn
Of such a wond'rous boy as Chatterton—
Her slander'd, starv'd, self-slain and deathless son!
And oh, if some ambitious youth aspire,
In this Torch-race, to speed the sacred fire,
Amid a hundred rivals, hot as he,
To win the goal of Immortality;
Outstripp'd, forgotten, let him know life lost—
Or ev'n a Victor—count the fearful cost!

Ah, why is such so oft the Poet's fate,
Belov'd, admir'd, honour'd—when too late!
Why such neglect while drawing vital breath,
To grant an apotheosis in Death?
Immortal wreathes, forsooth, of Laureate bay,
His woe-worn body mingling with cold clay,
Held o'er it by a grinning Skeleton,
That seems to say, Lo! what the Bard hath won!
Aye, hardly won, thro' wasting torture years,
With toil that never felt the dew of tears,
And heart-blood, dripping, amid scoffs and sneers!
But see, his hour is come, his fame is full;
Crown we his Tomb!   And wreathe with flow'rs
        his Skull!
For Bread, to make a happy Home his own,
He ask'd—in vain!   But we will give—a Stone!
Yet not, stern Scotia, thine the sole disgrace:
It seems an epidemic of our race,
That starves you living, to adorn your urns,
Camoens, Goldsmith, Chatterton, and Burns!
Perchance from man's ingratitude we draw
This recognition of a higher law;

The wreath of poet, hero, sage, to gain
Demands a life-apprenticeship to pain,
Labour, or penury; ought else in vain.
A Century now vouches for the pow'rs
Of Him, who needs no eulogy of ours;
To such the Muse her mystic web unrols,
They read the secrets of our inmost souls;
Live in the past, or view with prescient ken
The tendencies of worlds, as well as men;
Not chain'd to place and time, our poor abodes,
Such spirits, but for Passion's fearful odds,
Compar'd with other men, were Demigods!

Sadly we leave the Poet; sadly scan
The ruin'd Angel in the fallen Man!
Not that his Genius ever stoop'd to Crime;
His vices bore the stamp of Race and Clime;
They lur'd him on, like Sirens, to destroy,
Beneath the winsome masques of Love, and Joy:
The love of Woman, and the jovial glass,
That say to weary time—and sorrow—pass!
And oh, too fast they hurried Burns away,
Spurr'd by his wit, and feather'd by his lay,
Till he forgot how few the moments giv'n
To cleanse the Soul for Sabbaths of high Heav'n!
But pleasure's philtre acts upon the brain;
All libertines are more or less insane.
His heart—that still expanded, high and broad,
To it nought alien of the works of God,
The field mouse, mountain daisy, wounded hare,
All sure of sympathy—or shelter there—
His head—that seem'd, while going further wrong,
To find its lucid intervals in song—
His soul—in ruins—wearing such a grace
As made the Seraphs sigh o'er Belial's vacant place—
Their downward course—let others calmly tell,

Not one who can imagine it too well!
Let him, ne'er led astray by Woman's eyes,
Let him, 'mid festal wine-cups, always wise;
Who, while so many fall, can feel secure
That he shall stand, still temperate, and pure,
Be Judge of Burns, condemn his latter years!
For me—the Page were blotted out with tears:
By both his Genius, and his Passions, aw'd,
I leave him—to the Mercy of his God!

———

Dropping the veil upon the last sad scene,
A word anent his world-mistaken Jean.
"The plighted Husband of her youth" own'd her
By valid ties, although irregular;
Yet strangely blinded, his beclouded Life
Scarce recognized its wealth, in such a wife;
For sounder woman earth hath seldom seen,
In mind, or body, than that Bonny Jean;
Head with more sense, or heart with less disguise,
Song on her lips, and laughter in her eyes!
With wit enough her Burns to estimate,
And melody his lay to modulate,
And love to make his hearth a happy home;
Ah! what but madness from such love could roam,
False to himself and her!
                              She gently press'd
Another's offspring to her nursing breast,
And when some marvel'd whose the babe so fed,
"A neebor's bairn," was all Jean Armour said.
Oh! Priest and Levite, match me if ye can,
Such neighbourhood of this Samaritan!
To me it reads a conquest of high mark,
As ought recorded of brave Joan of Arc.
What heroism claims a higher prize

Than this wrong'd woman's pure self-sacrifice?
Strange, if such victories are often won,
That, save Griselda's, we remember none.
This *more* than wife was true, to her last breath,
To Burns alive, his memory in death;
A widow'd lot for lengthen'd years she pass'd,
His lover and defender to the last:
His merits to extol, his faults to screen,
Was one, aye ready—thou, oh Bonny Jean!
While He shall conquer time, and fame assume,
At least let scandal spare thy humble Tomb!

NOTES.

(¹) *Hangs o'er* GLENDALLOCH'S *hallow'd tow'r.*

GLENDALLOCH, or Glyn of the Double Lake, is situated in Wicklow, a County which presents "an abridgment of all that is pleasing in" Nature. This particular Glyn is surrounded on all sides, except to the East, by mountains, whose height throws a gloom on the vale below, well suited to inspire religious dread and horror. It has therefore been, from the most distant times, haunted with those spectres of illusive fancy which delight to hover in the gloom of ignorance and superstition. It is said to have been an asylum of the Druids, who fled from Roman tyranny. It was afterwards the refuge of the Monks, who established there a different religious rule, in which mind and body were bound in the same bondage of five years silence, severe fasts, obedience unto death; and this lake became their Dead Sea. Here, however, was the school of the West, an ark that preserved the remains of literature from the deluge of barbarism which overspread the rest of Europe. Here the ancient Britons took refuge from the Saxons, and the native Irish from the incursions of the Danes. On the round tower of Glendalloch was often blown the horn of war. Amidst a silent and melancholy waste, it still raises its head above the surrounding fragments, as if moralizing on the ruins of our country, and the wreck of its legislative independence. We think of MARIUS, when he said to the lictor, "Go and tell that you have seen Marius sitting on the *ruins* of Carthage!"—DR. D.

(²) *The cause, or the men, of the* EMERALD ISLE.

It may appear puerile to lay claim to a priority of application in the use of an epithet; but poets, like bees, have a very strong sense of property; and both are of that irritable kind, as to be extremely jealous of any one who robs them of their hoarded sweets. The sublime epithet which Milton used in his poem on the Nativity, written at fifteen years of age, ("his thunder-clasping hand,") would have been claimed by him as his own, even after he had finished the Paradise Lost. And Gray would prosecute as a literary poacher, the daring hand that would presume to break into his orchard, and appropriate a single epithet in that line, the most beautifully descriptive which ever was written—

"The breezy call of incense-breathing morn!"

On such authority, a poetaster reclaims the original use of an epithet—The EMERALD ISLE, in a party song, written without the rancour of party, in the year 1795. From the frequent use made of the term since that time, he fondly hopes that it will gradually become associated with the name of his country, as descriptive of its prime natural beauty, and its inestimable value.—DR. D.

(³) *Wake, page 46.—"A flung reward to human hounds."*

"This country," says the Earl of Essex, Lord Lieutenant in 1675, "has been perpetually rent and torn since his Majesty's Restoration. I can compare it to nothing better than the flinging the reward, on the death of the deer, among the pack of hounds, where every one pulls and tears where he can for himself."—ED.

(⁴) The author of the Familiar Epistles is not, I believe, certainly known. They were attributed very generally to John Wilson Croker, but I have lately seen this denied.—ED.

(⁵) Alluding to the tideless Mediterranean. The somewhat exaggerated gratitude of Abd-el-Kader did not quite respond to the character of the rhapsody. We cannot forget that his liberation was probably hastened by the generous efforts of an Irishman—the late Marquis of Londonderry.—ED.

JOHN FALCONER, Printer, 53, Upper Sackville-street, Dublin.

CPSIA information can be obtained at www.ICGtesting.com
Printed in the USA
LVOW08*2246200715

446916LV00011B/360/P